Magnificent
Jesus

CWR

Wendy Virgo

Contents

Introduction

In this series of studies for Lent we are going to consider some of the ways in which Jesus is described in the Gospel of John. This Gospel is rich in images which help us to understand some glorious aspects of the Son of God and the ways in which He meets the needs of lost, sinful and hopeless people. It was often in encounters with such people that Jesus unfolded a new aspect of His ministry; for example, to a blind man He comes as light, and to a women drawing water as One who can provide an eternal spring.

As the Gospel proceeds and we draw nearer to the cross, we find the concept of Jesus as the Lamb of God bearing away the sin of the world. This concept, which is introduced in the first chapter, becomes increasingly poignant. It is no longer just a concept; it is an amazing, powerful fact, and the actual fulfilment of Old Testament prophecy.

We can make all sorts of exciting discoveries about the life, death and resurrection of Jesus through stories and prophecies in the Old Testament. And so we will study some relevant passages in this book. Jesus Himself said, 'You diligently study the Scriptures because you think that by them you possess eternal life. These are the Scriptures that testify about me ...' (John 5:39). The Pharisees and other learned men held the books of Moses and the prophets as sacred documents, but failed to realise that they were not holy icons, but pointed the way to the One who would fulfil all the demands of the Law by living a holy life. Jesus declared, '*I am* the way and the truth and the life' (14:6, my emphasis).

One of the most enthralling things about the Bible is its consistency, the way it all hangs together. Some people wonder why we need the Old Testament – surely the revelation of Jesus in the Gospels and the subsequent preaching of the apostles in the New Testament are enough? They are certainly enough in the sense that in them we see Jesus bringing to us the good news about how we can be saved, by understanding that He is the Son of God who came to die the death that we deserve and to give us new life by His Spirit. But the Old Testament takes us on a wonderful journey, showing us why we need to be saved in the first place, and then gradually unfolding how this will happen. It is littered with beautiful clues describing the Person and the work of this magnificent Saviour. When we see, for example, in the Old Testament that a lamb was required to be sacrificed for sin, the account of John the Baptist proclaiming, as Jesus walks onto the scene, 'Look, the Lamb of God, who takes away the sin of the world!', suddenly takes on huge significance. History fills out the background for us, leaving us gasping at the intricate design and forethought of our heavenly Father, and His utter commitment to our salvation.

John the evangelist leads us through the events surrounding the death of Christ into the glorious truth of the resurrection, and so Jesus' statement, 'I am the resurrection and the life' (11:25), declared earlier to Martha and Mary, becomes liberating fact, preached by the apostles and evangelists of the Early Church and celebrated by all subsequent generations of believers.

As we prepare ourselves to visit again the events leading up to the death and resurrection of our Saviour, let us pray for the Holy Spirit to break in afresh into our busy lives to reveal something more of the mystery and majesty of the Christ who came to redeem us: out of aridity into refreshment; from emptiness to satisfaction; from darkness to light; from hopeless wandering to safety and security; from guilt and condemnation to salvation; and from death to life.

This is our God!

The Water of Life
John 4:1-30

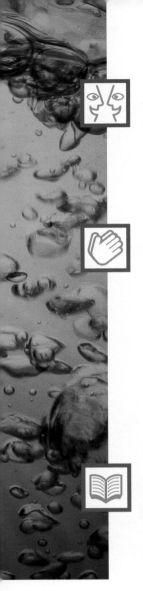

Icebreaker

Water is vital to life on our planet! It exists in solid, liquid and gaseous forms, covers 70% of the earth's surface and makes up 55 to 75% of the human body!

Pour a glass of water for each person. Before you begin to drink it, remind yourselves of the various ways in which water is so vital to our lives.

Opening Prayer

Father God, we come at this season of the year to focus again on Jesus, who lived and died and rose again that we might receive Your forgiveness and new life. We need to be constantly renewed and refreshed in our faith and in the awareness of Your unfailing love. Our spirits become dry and thirsty, and so we turn to You, the source of Living Water.

Thank You, Lord Jesus, that You invite us to come to You, just as we are. You know about our sins and failures, as You knew about the Samaritan woman's. Just as You revealed Yourself to her, please come and reveal Yourself afresh to us. Amen.

Bible Readings

Exodus 17:3–7

But the people were thirsty for water there, and they grumbled against Moses. They said, 'Why did you bring us up out of Egypt to make us and our children and livestock die of thirst?'
Then Moses cried to the LORD, 'What am I to do with these people? They are almost ready to stone me.'
The LORD answered Moses, 'Walk on ahead of the people. Take with you some of the elders of Israel and take in your hand the staff with which you struck the Nile, and go. I will stand there before you by the rock of Horeb. Strike the rock, and water will

come out of it for the people to drink.' So Moses did this in the sight of the elders of Israel. And he called the place Massah and Meribah because the Israelites quarrelled and because they tested the LORD saying, 'Is the LORD among us or not?'

John 4:13-14

Jesus answered, 'Everyone who drinks this water will be thirsty again, but whoever drinks the water I give him will never thirst. Indeed, the water I give him will become in him a spring of water welling up to eternal life.'

John 7:37-39

On the last and greatest day of the Feast, Jesus stood and said in a loud voice, 'If anyone is thirsty, let him come to me and drink. Whoever believes in me, as the Scripture has said, streams of living water will flow from within him.' By this he meant the Spirit, whom those who believed in him were later to receive. Up to that time the Spirit had not been given, since Jesus had not yet been glorified.

Revelation 22:1-2

Then the angel showed me the river of the water of life, as clear as crystal, flowing from the throne of God and of the Lamb down the middle of the great street of the city. On each side of the river stood the tree of life, bearing twelve crops of fruit, yielding its fruit every month. And the leaves of the tree are for the healing of the nations.

Eye Opener

The Bible is full of references to water, and it is often a metaphor for spiritual life. The prophet Jeremiah spoke the words of God when he said: 'My people have committed two sins: They have forsaken me, the spring of living water, and have dug their own cisterns, broken cisterns that cannot hold water' (Jer. 2:13). This was a constant complaint of the prophets: that God was the true source

of life, but they kept deserting Him to run after other gods, which were impotent and unable to slake their thirst.

What are human beings thirsty for? We are made in God's image. Therefore, deep down we need and crave things which pertain to God: love, purity, relational joy and completeness, peace and fulfilment. But, because of our sinful nature, instead of finding them in Him, we tend to look to other sources for our thirst to be assuaged. Everyone needs water to sustain life; without it, we die. The same is true spiritually. Our spirits can become dry, and faint – we need to come regularly to the fountain of life and drink.

Setting the Scene

Exodus 17:1-7; Numbers 20:1-13

Far back in the history of Israel, the rescued nation wandering through the desert was in desperate need of water. Moses and Aaron sought God on their behalf, and God told them to strike a rock and water would gush forth. Moses took his staff, struck the rock and water poured out, enough to meet the needs of two million people and their flocks and herds!

This is a beautiful picture foreshadowing the One who would become the Rock of Ages. In 1 Corinthians 10:4, Paul explicitly identifies the Rock with Jesus Christ. By bearing the guilt and penalty for the sin of all mankind, He would be struck by the rod of God's anger because of man's rebellion, and its terrible consequences. On the cross, from His side flowed physical blood and water. But also from this supreme act of sacrifice there now flows a never failing stream of 'living water': peace and joy in this life, and eternal life in the age to come. Jesus is our Rock, and the source of living water.

Later, in another time of drought, Moses was instructed to approach the rock again, but this time simply to speak to it. But he struck it in frustration, and for that was denied entry into the promised land. Why so severe a penalty?

Just as Moses only needed to strike the rock once, so Jesus, the Rock, was struck once and this bore away our sin for ever. Now we need only come to Him and ask and we will receive living water. We will see two instances in John's Gospel of Jesus offering living water to those who are inwardly thirsty. 'If anyone is thirsty, let him come to me and drink' (John 7:37). We only have to come to the Rock and ask!

Session Focus

John 4:1-30

She waited as long as possible, until no one else was likely to be around, before she swung the large jar up on her shoulder and set off for the well. She had her reasons for wanting to be alone: to avoid the accusing stares, the turned shoulders, the whispered comments. It would be another lonely day.

A man was sitting on the low wall. How annoying! She didn't want to speak to anyone. However, it would be unlikely a man would address a woman in public.

As she set down her jar by the well and began to let down the bucket, she realised by the style of the man's garment that He was a Jew. She was a Samaritan – Jews considered them unclean. Feeling even more uncomfortable, she kept her eyes resolutely lowered.

Then He spoke. He sounded tired. 'Will you give Me a drink?'

She stood up and looked at Him, frowning, puzzled.

'You are a Jew,' she stated baldly, 'and I am a Samaritan woman. How can You ask me for a drink?'

'If you knew who was speaking to you, you would have asked Him and He would have given you living water.'

This made no sense to her. He had no bucket; and what did 'living water' mean?

Then He said, 'Everyone who drinks this water will be thirsty again, but I can provide water that will satisfy thirst for ever. In fact, I can put a well of eternal life on

the inside that keeps springing up!'

He had her attention now! Such a well would be wonderfully convenient!

'Sir, give me this water so I won't have to keep coming here to draw water!'

His response took her aback completely.

'Go, call your husband and come back.'

This was tricky. Swiftly she deflected the demand, 'I have no husband.' 'You are right,' said Jesus. 'You have been married five times and are living with a man who is not your husband.'

This knowledge amazed her and she began to perceive that a supernatural element was at work here. 'You are a prophet,' she said. This man knew all about her, but He did not bully or condemn her. However, she was not ready to talk about her personal failures yet. She pushed them aside and introduced the more impersonal topic of religious friction. What about the Jew/Samaritan divide?

There are so many things happening here! First, the day is hot, the work is hard, the woman is ashamed – but she needs water. She is only expecting to draw water as usual, but something happens that changes her humdrum existence for ever.

Jesus skilfully uncovers that she not only needs physical water, but that she is in a relational, moral, spiritual desert. Her body needs water but her spirit is parched for real love, lasting relationship, and something which goes beyond religious correctness.

Gently, Jesus draws her out. He does not sidestep her question, but He does not allow Himself to be diverted by an argument about religion either. The woman follows His reasoning closely, acknowledging that the Christ will come. Imagine the rush of wonder when He states clearly, 'I who speak to you am he' (v.26). And she believes Him. Up till then, He had seemed to her just a man who was tired and thirsty; now she knows He is the Saviour of the world! Joyfully, she runs to take the good news to others.

John 7:37–39

The scene changes. Now we are in the Temple. It is at the end of the Feast of Tabernacles, and the high priest, intoning the Scriptures, pours a stream of water over the altar, recalling God's provision of water in the desert for a nation dying of thirst. This has become a sterile ritual, an impersonal, objective reminder of history. It appears to have no relevance in the lives of the bystanders. Afterwards they will drift off, with a vague feeling that there was something meritorious about observing an external ceremony. It won't change their hearts, but it somehow makes them 'feel good'.

Suddenly Jesus' voice rings out, startling in its urgency and clarity.

'If anyone is thirsty, let him come to Me and drink. Whoever believes in Me, as the Scripture has said, streams of living water will flow from within him.' What a bold claim!

It provoked a variety of reactions. Some, perhaps reminded of Moses' prophecy that another 'prophet like me' would arise, wonder if this is indeed the Prophet. Others say, 'He is the Christ.' Still others think He is a fraud and want Him arrested. But if any had run to Jesus and cried, 'I'm thirsty! Let me come and drink!' Jesus would have had to say, 'Not yet!'

When He spoke of the living water, He was referring to the Holy Spirit whom He would send after His death and resurrection. The Spirit would manifest the life that Jesus would make available for all who would come believing to Him.

Discussion Starters

1. Does commemoration of past significant events serve any useful purpose?

_____

_____

_____

_____

_____

2. What sorts of things might modern people be thirsty for?

_____

_____

_____

_____

_____

3. In what ways might you identify with the woman at the well, and the onlookers in the Temple?

_____

_____

_____

_____

_____

4. How did Jesus engage with the woman at the well?

_____

_____

_____

_____

5. Reading John 7:37–39, who can come and drink?

_____

_____

_____

_____

_____

6. How does the Holy Spirit deal with our 'soul thirst'?

_____

_____

_____

_____

_____

7. Look at John 4:6–7 and 19:28–30. Jesus knew what it was like to be thirsty. How can this realisation help us in our understanding of our magnificent Saviour?

_____

_____

_____

_____

_____

8. Have you responded to Jesus' invitation to come and drink?

_____

_____

_____

_____

_____

Final Thoughts

What are you thirsty for? Maybe you feel arid and dissatisfied. You have tried various diversions but are left feeling something is missing. So many things today compete for our attention, assuring us that they hold the key to satisfaction. But we neglect to care for our thirsty souls at our peril. Holidays, travel, eating, drinking, having fun with family and friends, sport, creativity, fulfilling work – these are all good gifts from the Father, who gives us richly all things to enjoy. But during this Lenten period, it will do us good to pause and take stock of the state of our spirits. Are they fully fed and watered? Are we full of faith and hope, rejoicing in the grace of God and in fellowship with Him? Or are we parched, longing for a good long drink of living water?

Let's take heed of Isaiah's words: 'Come, all you who are thirsty, come to the waters …!' (Isa. 55:1). We can come. Just as we are. Discontented, ashamed, feeling regretful for things done or not done, simply repentant, and believing that, as we draw near to Jesus, He will draw near to us and unlock the well.

I heard the voice of Jesus say:
'Behold I freely give
The living water, thirsty one,
Stoop down and drink and live.'
I came to Jesus, and I drank
Of that life-giving stream;
My thirst was quenched, my soul revived,
And now I live in Him.

Horatius Bonar (1808–1889)

Closing Prayer

Lord Jesus, thank You for Your offer of life-giving water, which quenches my soul thirst. I come to You to drink and will return day after day, knowing the source will never run dry. Amen.

The Bread of Life
John 6:25-71

Icebreaker

Bread is a staple food all over the world. How many different types of bread can you name? What is your favourite topping or filling?

Opening Prayer

Lord, we come to You, hungry to know You more. Teach us to find the energy, nourishment and satisfaction for our souls in You. Cause our hearts to burn within us as You speak to us, like the two disciples on the road to Emmaus. Amen.

Bible Readings

Exodus 16:2-4,13-16

In the desert the whole community grumbled against Moses and Aaron. The Israelites said to them, 'If only we had died by the LORD's hand in Egypt! There we sat round pots of meat and ate all the food we wanted, but you brought us out into this desert to starve this entire assembly to death.'

Then the LORD said to Moses, 'I will rain down bread from heaven for you. The people are to go out each day and gather enough for that day...' ...

That evening quail came and covered the camp, and in the morning, there was a layer of dew around the camp. When the dew was gone, thin flakes like frost on the ground appeared on the desert floor. When the Israelites saw it, they said to each other, 'What is it?' For they did not know what it was.

Moses said to them, 'It is the bread the LORD has given you to eat.'

Psalm 78:23-25

Yet he gave a command to the skies above
    and opened the doors of the heavens;

> he rained down manna for the people to eat,
>   he gave them the grain of heaven.
> Men ate the bread of angels;
>   he sent them all the food they could eat.

John 6:35,47-51

> Then Jesus declared, 'I am the bread of life. He who comes to me will never go hungry, and he who believes in me will never be thirsty …
> 'I tell you the truth, he who believes has everlasting life. I am the bread of life. Your forefathers ate the manna in the desert, yet they died. But here is the bread that comes down from heaven, which a man may eat and not die. I am the living bread that came down from heaven. If anyone eats of this bread, he will live for ever. This bread is my flesh, which I will give for the life of the world.'

Eye Opener

Jesus said, 'I am the bread of life' (John 6:35). Let's see how events in the Old Testament point towards the Saviour who could claim this. Again, we go back to the wandering of the Israelites in the wilderness. They have been delivered from slavery, but soon the euphoria dies away to be replaced by the practical concerns of life: they have no food! Panic sets in, and they pour out their complaints to Moses. God speaks to Moses and tells him, 'I will rain down bread from heaven for you. The people are to go out each day and gather enough for that day' (Exod. 16:4). In the morning, a white substance covered the ground, the promised bread. 'The people of Israel called the bread manna. It was white like coriander seed and tasted like wafers made with honey' (v.31).

Notice that in spite of their grumbling, God provided for them lavishly. He 'rained' it down! It went on for forty years, a continual supply for as long as they needed it.

Setting the Scene

John 6

The hillside was covered with people as far as the eye could see. They had been there all day, avidly listening to Jesus' teaching and then pressing around Him for His healing touch. The mood was happy and excited; but now, as daylight began to fade, babies could be heard crying, and little children were sleepily protesting, 'I'm hungry, Mamma!'

Jesus turned to Philip, who came from nearby Bethsaida. 'Where shall we buy food for them, Philip?'

Philip recoiled in shock. What was *he* supposed to do? It would cost a fortune!

Then Andrew came up, holding a little boy by the hand. His voice was full of amusement as he said, 'This little guy is offering his lunch! But it's only five rolls and a couple of sardines! That's not going to go far amongst this lot!'

Jesus didn't laugh, but He smiled warmly at the lad, and took the proffered bag. He turned to the disciples and told them to organise everyone into groups. Holding up a roll, He gave thanks. Then He began tearing off bits of bread and fish, and gave them to the disciples to distribute. The astonishing thing was that for every bit Jesus tore off there always seemed to be more! The food did not diminish, it multiplied!

Well over 5,000 people stuffed themselves! It was such a lavish picnic that the grass was littered with leftovers, which the disciples piled into twelve overflowing baskets.

The excited crowd began clamouring for Jesus to be their king, but He withdrew from them.

The next day, they found Him. Jesus looked at them and said, in effect, 'You enjoyed it when I fed you, and you want Me to keep on supplying your material needs. But you have not understood the significance. There is another food which brings eternal satisfaction.'

Session Focus

John 6:25-71

Next day, the people were struggling to understand Him. They were still hung up on asking for signs, while not comprehending the miracle they had witnessed. They made the link with Moses and the manna in the wilderness, but still thought in material terms. Now Jesus says, '… the bread of God is he who comes down from heaven and gives life to the world' (v.33).

Like the woman at the well, they responded, thinking in terms of their own convenience: 'From now on give us this bread!' (v.34).

Jesus Himself had resisted the temptation to focus on merely satisfying physical hunger when there was a more serious issue at stake (Matt. 4:1–11). He was a man, and understood and experienced human hunger, but quoted back to the devil from Deuteronomy, 'Man does not live on *bread* alone, but on every *word* that comes from the mouth of God' (v.4, my emphasis).

Often the Word of God is spoken of as 'food' or 'bread'. In the first chapter of John's Gospel, Jesus is spoken of as the *logos*, translated 'the Word'. Hebrews echoes this, '… in these last days, he [God] has spoken to us by his Son …' (1:1). To look at Jesus is to know what God has said, about Himself, about sin, about the world, about us. He expresses all the Father's love, and will, and Person, in a body of flesh.

Now Jesus puts it in a different way: 'I am the bread of life' (John 6:35). What does bread signify? It speaks of nourishment, of sustaining life, of satisfaction. It speaks of the basic necessities for maintaining strength and health. We talk of 'putting bread on the table'; the normality of life, without frills or excesses. Cake is for some, bread is for all.

Jesus was saying, 'I am what you need to maintain spiritual life. If you believe in Me, you can receive Me, take My life into the core of your being, and allow My strength

to empower you and energise you, not for your human desires, but to fulfil My desires through you.' Jesus said His food was 'to do the will of him who sent me' (John 4:34).

Jesus' pronouncement, 'I am the bread of life. He who comes to me will never go hungry, and he who believes in me will never be thirsty', is beautiful in its simplicity and economy, yet it encapsulates profound and sublime truth. A child can grasp the essence that Jesus is all he needs, yet the greatest minds can never fully comprehend all the depths implied in it.

All other bread, like the manna in the wilderness, leaves a sense of dissatisfaction – we get hungry again. But Jesus assuages the deep hunger of our spirits. As the psalmist said, 'Taste and see that the LORD is good' (Psa. 34:8).

As we prepare ourselves for Easter, our minds must go to the cross as we see the significance of Jesus' words: 'This bread is my flesh, which I will give for the life of the world' (John 6:51).

His hearers found this distasteful: 'How can this man give us his flesh to eat?' (v.52). Jesus did not moderate His language, but went further: 'Whoever eats my flesh and drinks my blood has eternal life, and I will raise him up at the last day' (v.54). This was even more repulsive!

Yet, for those who have ears to hear, these are truly words of life; timeless in their application; boundless in their scope. What revelation! As we contemplate the Son of God hanging bleeding and broken upon the cross, we see His body is indeed bread for the world. For those who come humbly to Him, declaring their belief, we 'eat' of Him, secure that our souls will receive eternal life – we shall never die!

Not only that; we can 'eat' of Him every day, chewing on His truth, nourishing our minds on His words, strengthened, sustained, kept, energised, guided and envisioned as the Holy Spirit comes alongside, as Jesus said He would, to 'remind you of everything I have said to you' (John 14:26).

Let us respond using Peter's declaration:
'Lord, to whom shall we go? You have the words of
eternal life. We believe and know that you are the
Holy One of God' (John 6:68).

Discussion Starters

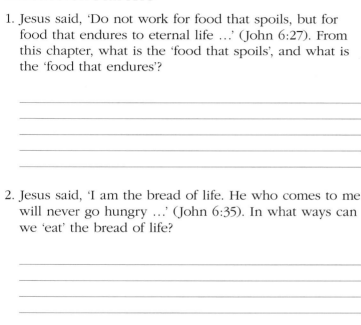

1. Jesus said, 'Do not work for food that spoils, but for
   food that endures to eternal life ...' (John 6:27). From
   this chapter, what is the 'food that spoils', and what is
   the 'food that endures'?

   _____

   _____

   _____

   _____

   _____

2. Jesus said, 'I am the bread of life. He who comes to me
   will never go hungry ...' (John 6:35). In what ways can
   we 'eat' the bread of life?

   _____

   _____

   _____

   _____

   _____

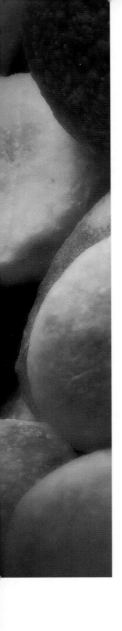

3. Jesus said, '… I have come down from heaven not to do my will but to do the will of him who sent me' (John 6:38). What was the will of the Father?

_____

_____

_____

_____

_____

4. Jesus said, 'I tell you the truth, he who believes has everlasting life. I am the bread of life' (John 6:47–48). What do you think Jesus was saying here about 'life'?

_____

_____

_____

_____

_____

5. In what way do we become spiritually hungry? How can Jesus satisfy us?

_____

_____

_____

_____

_____

6. Jesus' hearers found His sayings 'hard' (John 6:60). Have you found some of His teaching hard? Hard to understand? Or hard to follow?

_____

_____

_____

_____

_____

7. In John 6:66–70 we see the challenge of following Jesus. His truth can be hard to understand and hard to apply, our loyalty can be tested, and we can find ourselves part of a minority group. What difficulties have you experienced as you have sought to follow Jesus?

_____

_____

_____

_____

_____

8. '… unless a grain of wheat falls to the ground and dies, it remains only a single seed. But if it dies, it produces many seeds' (John 12:24). Read the whole passage. What are the contrasts?

_____

_____

_____

_____

_____

Final Thoughts

In the account of the Last Supper in John's Gospel, Jesus focuses His teaching on the coming Holy Spirit, but in the synoptic Gospels we have a clear account of Him taking bread and breaking it, saying, 'This is my body given for you; do this in remembrance of me' (Luke 22:19; Matt. 26:26; Mark 14:22). Paul also refers to it in 1 Corinthians 11:23. Jesus was very deliberate about instituting a way of perpetual remembrance. This is, therefore, very important for us. His statement, 'I am the bread of life' was supremely pointing forward to the cross, when He would literally be broken.

'Then Pilate took Jesus and had him flogged. The

soldiers twisted together a crown of thorns and put it on his head … Finally Pilate handed him over to be crucified … Carrying his own cross, he went out to the place of the Skull … Here they crucified him' (John 19:1–2,16–18). Jesus knew that this terrible, brutal death was His destiny. He was born in Bethlehem, which means 'house of bread'. That small insignificant town was the place from which bread came to feed the world.

Let us take bread now, break it and share it together, and bow in wonder that redemption, forgiveness, healing and salvation are available to us as we remember and receive Jesus, our Bread of Life.

Break Thou the Bread of Life,
Dear Lord, to me,
As Thou didst break the bread
Beside the sea;
Beyond the sacred page
I seek Thee, Lord,
My spirit longs for Thee,
Thou Living Word.

Bless Thou the Truth, dear Lord
To me, to me,
As Thou didst bless the loaves
By Galilee;
Then shall all bondage cease,
All fetters fall,
And I shall find my peace,
My all in all.

Mary Lathbury (1841–1913)

Closing Prayer

Lord Jesus, when we come to You, we truly find that a deep hunger within is satisfied. Thank You for giving Your body to be broken that we might be made whole. Keep persuading us that You can provide all that we need, in this life and the next! Amen.

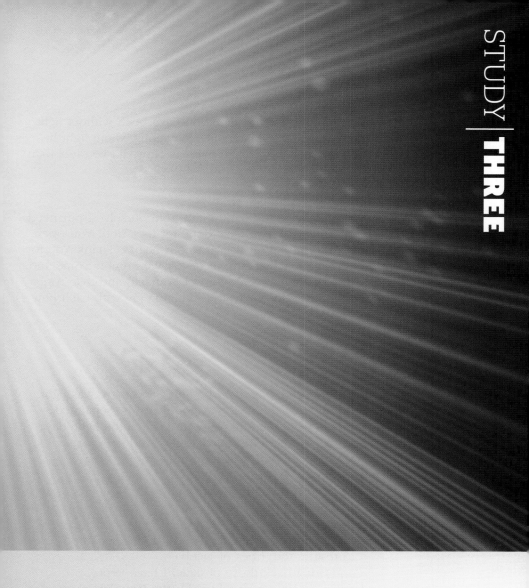

The Light of the World
John 9:1-41

Icebreaker

Share some situations when you have been without light. How did you feel? Share some situations where light has been extremely bright and intense. How did you feel then?

Opening Prayer

Father, we are in the dark about You, ourselves, our need of You and what You have done for us – until You open our eyes, bringing revelation to our hearts. Thank You for the light we have already received. We humbly come and ask that You will reveal more of Yourself, and that Your light will blaze in our hearts, bringing joy with each new discovery. Amen.

Bible Readings

Genesis 1:3–5
And God said, 'Let there be light,' and there was light. God saw that the light was good, and he separated the light from the darkness. God called the light 'day', and the darkness he called 'night'. And there was evening, and there was morning – the first day.

Psalm 27:1
The LORD is my light and my salvation –
whom shall I fear?

Isaiah 49:6
'It is too small a thing for you to be my servant
to restore the tribes of Jacob
and bring back those of Israel I have kept.
I will also make you a light for the Gentiles,
that you may bring my salvation to the ends of
the earth.'

Isaiah 60:1–3
'Arise, shine, for your light has come,
and the glory of the LORD rises upon you.
See, darkness covers the earth

and thick darkness is over the peoples,
but the LORD rises upon you
   and his glory appears over you.
Nations will come to your light,
   and kings to the brightness of your dawn.'

John 1:4-5

In him was life, and that life was the light of men.
The light shines in the darkness, but the darkness
has not understood it.

John 3:19-21

'... Light has come into the world, but men loved
darkness instead of light because their deeds were
evil. Everyone who does evil hates the light, and will
not come into the light for fear that his deeds will be
exposed. But whoever lives by the truth comes into
the light, so that it may be seen plainly that what he
has done has been done through God.'

John 8:12

Jesus ... said, 'I am the light of the world. Whoever
follows me will never walk in darkness, but will have
the light of life.'

Eye Opener

Perhaps you have been in an aeroplane at night and
looked out of the window, and seen ... nothing. But then
it's as if someone takes a pen and draws a golden streak
across the formless expanse. Gradually the streak widens
and flames into crimson and orange. The beauty of dawn
lights up the horizon.

The first thing God created was light. God spoke.
Light appeared: 'Through him all things were made ...
In him was life, and that life was the light of men. The
light shines in the darkness, but the darkness has not
understood it' (John 1:3–5). Light is so fundamental to us,
so necessary.

We hate to be in the dark; darkness is dangerous; we
bump into things, fall into holes, walk into walls. We fear

the dark because nameless things may be lurking there. We feel vulnerable; we are potential victims of accidents or crimes such as theft or violence. We associate darkness with caverns and dungeons, with despondency, sadness and ignorance.

Yet the Bible says that 'men loved darkness instead of light because their deeds were evil' (John 3:19–21). Here the word 'light' means the knowledge of God. Many would rather remain in ignorance than risk exposure and shame. But when God's light flames into our hearts, it changes everything!

 Setting the Scene

Light is a constant theme in the Bible, from Genesis to Revelation. God began creation with light, and in heaven 'There will be no more night. They will not need the light of a lamp or the light of the sun, for the Lord God will give them light' (Rev. 22:5). The Old Testament abounds with references to light meaning knowledge, and especially knowledge of God.

The Israelites were guided through the wilderness by the pillar of cloud by day and the pillar of fire by night. A seven-branched candlestick stood in the tabernacle, and later in the Temple. Then all through the Psalms there are joyful references to God being and giving light: '… my God turns my darkness into light' (Psa. 18:28); 'The LORD is my light and my salvation …' (Psa. 27:1). Especially, we find light is a theme in Isaiah. God's promise to give light to Israel widens to include Gentiles, and to 'the ends of the earth' (Isa. 49:6). The Messiah is awaited as the One who will 'open the eyes that are blind' (Isa. 42:7), both literally and figuratively.

So John's beautiful opening verses to his Gospel are rich with meaning as he speaks of the 'word' being with God at creation, and being the light which has come into the darkness, in fact has been 'made flesh'.

It is poignant that a custom at the time of the Feast of

Tabernacles was to light huge lamps in the Temple courts, and the people would celebrate by singing and dancing through the night. The blind man, sitting nearby, could not see the light. But the celebrating people were also blind in their ignorance that the 'light of the world' was among them.

This is the background to the healing of the blind man, one of the signs that Jesus truly is the Messiah and our Saviour who enlightens our darkness.

Session Focus

John 9:1-41

He was used to connecting to the world around him through sound and touch, not through sight. He had never seen, being congenitally afflicted with blindness. He had learnt to live with it; the only way in which he could support himself was to beg. Around the time of the Feast of Tabernacles, as he was sitting as usual, begging, he became aware of a group of people approaching. A voice said, 'Rabbi, why is this man blind? Did he or his parents sin?'

He was used to people talking over him as though he wasn't there.

He thought it an unfair question: how could he have sinned in the womb? He waited. 'Neither,' was the rabbi's reply. That was all right then! It wasn't his fault, or his parents'! But what came next was a big surprise.

'The work of God is going to be displayed in his life. While I have time, I must do God's work: soon it will be night, but while I am here, I am the light of the world.'

Before he could begin to understand these puzzling words, he heard someone spit on the ground. Then something soft and squashy and warm was gently smeared onto his sightless eye sockets: unexpected, but not unpleasant.

A hand helped him to his feet, and the same voice – presumably the rabbi's – said, 'Go and wash in the pool of Siloam.'

He knew it was nearby. So, grabbing his stick, he tapped his way over the cobblestones and round the corner. By the time he arrived at the pool, the clay had dried on his eyes. He felt his way to the edge and, leaning carefully over the low wall, began to splash water on his face. The dried mud came away. As his eyelids flickered open, an entirely new sensation came to him: light entered his experience, shapes, forms, colours presented themselves. He could see! Dizzy with wonder, shouting, he turned and stumbled back, hoping to meet the rabbi and His followers.

A crowd was collecting around him. 'Hey, it's the blind beggar!'

'No, it can't be, this fellow can see.'

'Well, he looks just like him.'

'It really is me!' he insisted.

'What happened? How come you are seeing?' they demanded.

'A man called Jesus made some mud, put it on my eyes, and told me to go and wash it off in the pool. So I did, and now I can see!'

Sadly, the man's parents were afraid of the Pharisees, others were sceptical, and the Pharisees themselves were plainly hostile. They were so concerned with external correctness that they failed to see the wonder and significance of such a miracle. In fact, they felt threatened by it and threw the ex-blind man out of the Temple. Jesus found him, and asked, 'Do you believe in the Son of Man?'

'Who is he, Sir?'

'You have seen Him; it is He who is speaking to you.' The man said, 'Lord, I believe,' and worshipped Him.

How wonderful that Jesus could say, 'You have seen Him!' He had 'seen' Jesus more profoundly than those whose physical eyes had not been impaired. Everyone who believes in Jesus can say, 'Once I was blind, but now I can see!', and the only appropriate response is to worship Him.

The healing was an act of compassion; but it was also deeply symbolic of the mission of the Messiah – to bring light into darkness. Paul wrote to the Corinthians, 'The god of this age has blinded the minds of unbelievers ...' (2 Cor. 4:4). Without illumination we remain in ignorance of our need of Jesus, of our fallen state, of who Jesus is, and of why He came. We do not understand the point of His death, or His resurrection. But revelation floods our souls when God makes 'his light shine in our hearts to give us the light of the knowledge of the glory of God in the face of Christ' (v.6).

The blind man who was healed literally looked into that face with newly opened eyes. We are not yet able to do that, but as we receive the good news of the gospel, light floods our souls and we feel the warmth of His love and the sense of His presence. Our spiritual eyes are opened!

Discussion Starters

1. When were your eyes first opened to see Jesus as your Saviour? And what immediate difference did it make to you?

_____

_____

_____

_____

_____

2. Have there been times when the light of Jesus has shone into an area you would rather have kept in the dark?

_____

_____

_____

_____

_____

3. Why do you think not everyone wants to admit the entrance of the light?

4. In what ways does God bring light into our lives?

5. Psalm 36:9 says, 'in your light we see light'. What do you think this means?

6. Psalm 119:105 says, 'Your word is a lamp to my feet and a light for my path.' Can you recall occasions when God's Word has brought particular illumination or guidance to you?

7. Read Matthew 5:14–16. In what ways can we be light in the world?

_____

_____

_____

_____

_____

Final Thoughts

The beauty of God's plans and purposes is that He intended His light to be shed all over the world! He calls us to be part of His mission to make Himself known. As Paul says, 'For *you* were once darkness, but now *you* are light in the Lord' (Eph. 5:8, my emphasis). As we live in the light of what Jesus has done for us, we become demonstrations of His light. It shines through us too. When Jesus died, it appeared that the light had been extinguished. But when He rose from the dead, light blazed forth! The more who come to the knowledge of the truth, the more the light shines.

Closing Prayer

Open my eyes, that I may see
Glimpses of truth Thou hast for me;
Place in my hands the wonderful key
That shall unclasp and set me free.
Silently now I wait for Thee,
Ready, my God, Thy will to see.
Open my eyes, illumine me, Spirit divine!
Clara H. Scott (1841–1897)

The Good Shepherd
John 10:1-18

Icebreaker

Blindfold a volunteer, spin them around a few times, and ask another volunteer to guide them through a set course using only his or her voice. The course could be simply a few chairs positioned at various points in a room or more elaborate if you have time and space! Other group members can all talk at the same time to make it harder for the blindfolded person to pick out the 'shepherd's' voice.

Opening Prayer

Father God, we acknowledge that often we behave like sheep: we are prone to wander; we don't like to stand out and be different, but instead bunch up with the rest of the flock; we don't learn from our mistakes!

But You are a shepherd who tenderly cares for the sheep, guards, guides and feeds them. Please continue to shepherd us; discipline us when we need it, defend us from the enemy who prowls around us, and teach us to hear Your voice. Amen.

Bible Readings

Psalm 23:1-6

The LORD is my shepherd, I shall not be in want.
  He makes me lie down in green pastures,
he leads me besides quiet waters,
  he restores my soul.
He guides me in paths of righteousness
  for his name's sake.
Even though I walk
  through the valley of the shadow of death,
I will fear no evil
  for you are with me;
your rod and your staff,
  they comfort me.

You prepare a table before me
in the presence of my enemies.
You anoint my head with oil;
my cup overflows.
Surely, goodness and love will follow me
all the days of my life,
and I will dwell in the house of the LORD
for ever.

Isaiah 40:11

He tends his flock like a shepherd:
He gathers the lambs in his arms
and carries them close to his heart;
he gently leads those that have young.

Ezekiel 34:1-2

The word of the LORD came to me: 'Son of man,
prophesy against the shepherds of Israel; prophesy
and say to them: "This is what the Sovereign LORD
says: Woe to the shepherds of Israel who only take
care of themselves! Should not shepherds take care
of the flock?"'

John 10:1-11

'I tell you the truth, the man who does not enter the
sheep pen by the gate, but climbs in by some other
way, is a thief and a robber. The man who enters by
the gate is the shepherd of his sheep. The watchman
opens the gate for him, and the sheep listen to his
voice. He calls his own sheep by name and leads
them out. When he has brought out all his own, he
goes on ahead of them, and his sheep follow him
because they know his voice. But they will never
follow a stranger; in fact, they will run away from
him because they do not recognise a stranger's
voice.' Jesus used this figure of speech, but they did
not understand what he was telling them.
Therefore Jesus said again, 'I tell you the truth, I am
the gate for the sheep. All who ever came before
me were thieves and robbers, but the sheep did not
listen to them. I am the gate; whoever enters through

me will be saved. He will come in and go out, and find pasture. The thief comes only to steal and kill and destroy; I have come that they may have life, and have it to the full.
I am the good shepherd. The good shepherd lays down his life for the sheep.'

Revelation 7:17
'For the Lamb at the centre of the throne will be their shepherd;
he will lead them to springs of water.
And God will wipe away every tear from their eyes.'

Eye Opener

A shepherd is someone who cares for his flock day and night, summer and winter, through drought or storm. He assists the ewes when they give birth; he searches the fleeces for ticks; he turns the sheep over when they have fallen helplessly on their backs; he keeps them from wandering into danger. The work can be tiring and demanding, but also humdrum, menial and dirty. The shepherd knows his sheep.

In the Old Testament, God repeatedly speaks of Israel as His flock and of Himself as their Shepherd, guarding, guiding, feeding and tending them. It is a gentle, domestic picture, conveying that the intimate bond between shepherd and sheep is what God desires with His people.

Setting the Scene

Israel's greatest king, David, was a shepherd boy. Perhaps one of the best-known pieces of literature in the world is the twenty-third psalm, which David wrote out of his experience of shepherding his sheep. Notice what elements of a shepherd's heart are alluded to in this psalm: leading, providing, tending, nourishing, admonishing, defending, protecting – all the way to the desired destination.

This is in sharp contrast to Ezekiel 34, where God denounces the false shepherds who do not have the interests of the sheep at heart.

Many of the Old Testament prophets speak of One to come who will be a 'good shepherd', One who truly cares for His flock even at the risk to His own life. Moses was a shepherd when God called him in the wilderness; David was a shepherd when Samuel anointed him to be king. They foreshadow a shepherd who would be a leader, a deliverer, a king: a shepherd who would surpass them.

Jesus' parable in Luke 15 is about a shepherd who has 100 sheep. One could suppose that out of such a crowd, if one went missing, it would not be a huge loss. But the shepherd is concerned for each individual sheep, and searches until he finds the one which went missing. Then, for sheer joy, he carries it back on his shoulders to the rest of the flock, calling fellow shepherds to rejoice with him. This speaks so eloquently of Jesus' love for even the rebellious sheep and His intention for it to be reunited with the flock; and of the grace of God that the returning prodigal is the object of the shepherd's delight.

Session Focus

John 10:1-18

A shepherd would have been a familiar figure in New Testament times. Most households would have had a few sheep, and in the village there would have been a fold, a walled enclosure, where sheep would be penned at night, perhaps several different flocks in one fold. In the morning, the shepherds would come to lead out their sheep. They would have their own distinctive calls and pet names which the sheep would recognise. So each shepherd would call out his own flock.

The fold had one doorway; anyone attempting to get in over the wall would not be a shepherd, but a robber. At this point Jesus says quite emphatically that all who came before Him were not true shepherds; only He is the

Good Shepherd. This discourse follows on directly from the previous chapter, where Jesus announces Himself as the light of the world. The scribes and Pharisees, who see themselves as the 'shepherds' of Israel, are incensed against Him, seeing Him as a schismatic Sabbath breaker. They are like the false shepherds of Ezekiel 34. They do not really care for the sheep and have only self-interest at heart.

But Jesus is different. His allegory alludes to several beautiful characteristics of a *good* Shepherd. *Firstly,* the sheep know Him and He knows His sheep. He calls them personally, by name. They recognise His voice and trust Him, and follow Him. He never drives, but leads them.

Secondly, the Greek word translated 'good' is *kalos* which carries in it the sense of 'worthy', 'true', 'noble'. The shepherd's job could be hard and dangerous, a rugged outdoor occupation which might involve defending the sheep from predators such as wolves, as well as thieves.

Thirdly, the shepherd brings security and freedom to His flock. He pens them up at night, guards them and then leads them out in the morning to find pasture. He provides for their wellbeing. They can 'come in and go out' (v.9). Under His supervision there is freedom but also safety. In fact, life under His care is 'abundant' (v.10)! This conjures up a picture of fat, contented sheep, munching away on the best grass, beside plenteous pools of water, untroubled by predators.

Fourthly, His commitment extends to laying down His life for them (v.11). This is the ultimate expression of care. Here is an explicit reference to Jesus' own death. He will not just accidentally lose His life – He will intentionally 'lay it down'. He loves the sheep so much that He will defend them, and lose His own life to save them. Later, Paul would write to the Ephesians, 'Christ loved the church and gave himself up for her' (Eph. 5:25).

The metaphor changes in John 10 verse 7. Jesus says, 'I am the gate for the sheep'. How can He be the gate or door, and the shepherd at the same time? H.V. Morton, in his book called *In the Steps of the Master*, describes a visit to Bethlehem. He got into conversation with a shepherd, who showed him a typical sheepfold. It was a snug, stone enclosure with only one entrance.

Morton remarked, 'There is no door.'

The shepherd replied, 'I am the door.'

He explained that He himself lay across the gap at night, so that any thief or predator would have to go through Him to get in. He was the only way in!

Jesus looked forward to a time when He would welcome 'other sheep' into His fold: 'I must bring them also. They too will listen to my voice, and there shall be one flock and one shepherd' (v.16). He was referring to those who were born outside the Jewish heritage, but who would believe in Him. They were once excluded. They were 'foreigners to the covenants of the promise, without hope and without God' (Eph. 2:12). But now in Christ we 'have been brought near through the blood of Christ … he has made the two one …' (vv.13–14). Jesus is the only way, whether for Jew or Gentile, to enter the fold.

Discussion Starters

1. Turn to Psalm 23. Verse 1 says, '... I shall not be in want.' In what ways does the Lord, our Shepherd, provide for us?

_____

_____

_____

_____

_____

2. 'He makes me lie down in green pastures ...' (Psa. 23:2). Does this mean the Christian life is one of ease and comfort?

_____

_____

_____

_____

_____

3. 'He guides me in paths of righteousness for his name's sake' (Psa. 23:3). What are these paths?

_____

_____

_____

_____

_____

4. Read verse 4 of Psalm 23 Perhaps you have walked through this dark valley; through bereavement or maybe a life-threatening situation. How did you feel? Did you find the presence of the Shepherd with you?

_____

_____

_____
_____
_____

5. Psalm 23 verse 4. What do you think the 'rod' and 'staff' signify?

_____
_____
_____
_____
_____

6. John 10:4 tells us that the sheep recognise the shepherd's voice. In what ways have you heard the Good Shepherd speak to you?

_____
_____
_____
_____
_____

7. 'When Jesus … saw a large crowd, he had compassion on them, because they were like sheep without a shepherd' (Mark 6:34). What did Jesus then do about this? Why is this important?

_____
_____
_____
_____
_____

8. Hebrews 13:20 says that Jesus is 'that great Shepherd of the sheep'. He is the model for pastors or, literally, shepherds. How can a modern 'pastor' emulate Jesus in serving the people of God?

_____

_____

_____

_____

_____

Final Thoughts

After the resurrection, Jesus met with the disciples on the beach of Lake Galilee. There He had a private conversation with Peter, in which He asked him three times to care for His flock. Later, in his first epistle, Peter twice referred to Jesus as 'the Shepherd'. Echoing Isaiah 53 he wrote, 'For you were like sheep going astray, but now you have returned to the Shepherd and Overseer of your souls' (1 Pet. 2:25). Then, as he gave instructions to the elders of the churches, he said, 'Be shepherds of God's flock that is under your care, serving as overseers … being examples to the flock. And when the Chief Shepherd appears, you will receive the crown of glory …' (1 Pet. 5:2–4). So Jesus provided the model for the pastors in the Early Church to follow. They were not to be greedy, not 'lording it' over the sheep, but serving them. Being a pastor was not to be seen as a means of getting prestige or riches. Jesus was the servant leader, and that continues to be the standard for us today. What an example: a Shepherd of supreme humility and unselfishness and love. Don't you love Him?

The King of Love my Shepherd is,
Whose goodness faileth never;
I nothing lack if I am His
And He is mine for ever ...

Perverse and foolish oft I strayed,
But yet in love He sought me,
And on His shoulder gently laid,
And home rejoicing brought me ...

Henry Williams Baker (1821–1877)

Closing Prayer

Lord Jesus, I am so glad You are my Shepherd! Thank You for Your constant care, for guiding, guarding, feeding and protecting me. But especially, I am amazed and humbled that You should lay down Your life for the sheep, for me. Amen.

STUDY | FIVE

The Lamb of God
John 1:29-34

Icebreaker

A lamb: small, dependent, weak, innocent. A mighty God, Creator of all things, also spoken of as a lion. Can you think of other contrasting ways in which Jesus is described?

Opening Prayer

Father God, please open our eyes to understand how our Saviour had to humble Himself to become a man, a baby, a lamb; to be willing to be despised, treated with contempt, and be condemned to death so that we might be saved. Amen.

Bible Readings

Genesis 22:7

Isaac spoke up and said to his father Abraham, 'Father?'
'Yes, my son,' Abraham replied.
'The fire and wood are here,' Isaac said, 'but where is the lamb for the burnt offering?'
Abraham answered, 'God himself will provide the lamb for the burnt offering, my son.' And the two of them went on together.

Exodus 12:3,5-8,11-14

'... each man is to take a lamb for his family, one for each household ... The animals you choose must be year-old males without defect ... the community of Israel must slaughter them at twilight. Then they are to take some of the blood and put it on the sides and tops of the door-frames of the houses where they eat the lambs. That same night they are to eat the meat roasted over the fire, along with bitter herbs, and bread made without yeast ... Eat it in haste; it is the LORD's Passover.
'On that same night I will pass through Egypt and strike down every firstborn – both men and animals

– and I will bring judgment on all the gods of Egypt. I am the Lord. The blood will be a sign for you on the houses where you are; and when I see the blood, I will pass over you. No destructive plague will touch you when I strike Egypt.
'This is a day you are to commemorate; for the generations to come ...'

Isaiah 53:6-7

We all, like sheep, have gone astray,
   each of us has turned to his own way;
and the Lord has laid on him
   the iniquity of us all.
He was oppressed and afflicted,
   yet he did not open his mouth;
he was led like a lamb to the slaughter,
   and as a sheep before her shearers is silent,
   so he did not open his mouth.

John 1:29-36

The next day John saw Jesus coming towards him and said, 'Look, the Lamb of God, who takes away the sin of the world! This is the one I meant when I said, "A man who comes after me has surpassed me because he was before me."'

Revelation 5:11-12

Then I looked and heard the voice of many angels, numbering thousands upon thousands, and ten thousand times ten thousand. They encircled the throne and the living creatures and the elders. In a loud voice they sang:
'Worthy is the Lamb, who was slain, to receive power and wealth and wisdom and strength and honour and glory and praise!'

Eye Opener

Sacrifice was introduced very early in the Bible. Noah sacrificed to God out of gratitude when the flood subsided; Abraham sacrificed at strategic points in his journey, and so

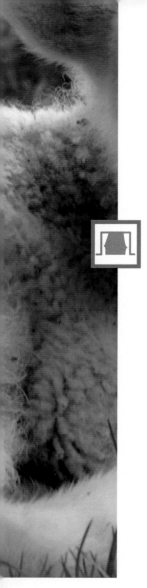

did Jacob. In the wilderness years, Moses set up the detailed system of sacrifices by which the sins of the people were dealt with. This became intricately woven into the rhythm of their lives and was the only way by which they could draw near to God. It should have been accompanied by true heart repentance, but became reduced to an external ritual which did not touch their hearts. But it all pointed forward to a Person, humble and innocent as a lamb.

Setting the Scene

Three scenes:

1. An old man and his son trudge slowly up a mountain track. The old man carries a container of smoking charcoal, swinging on a chain. Tucked into his belt is a knife, and over his shoulder a coil of rope. The teenage lad has a prickly bundle of firewood on his back. The sun beats down as they make their way to the summit. 'Father,' says the boy. 'We have wood and fire, but where is the lamb?' The old man looks at him tenderly, and the boy, wondering, sees tears in his eyes. 'God will provide a lamb,' says his father. They walk on to the top of the mountain. There they gather rocks and build an altar and lay the sticks on it. Then the man takes the rope and binds the boy's hands and feet, and lays him on the altar. The boy's eyes are dark with shock and terror. Abraham grasps his knife and sweeps it up in the air ready to plunge it into his son's heart. A voice rings out. 'Abraham! Do not kill your son! Now I know you fear God seeing that you have not withheld your only son from Me.' The tears now overflow as Abraham shakily helps Isaac off the altar. They hear a bleat: a ram is caught by its horns in a bush nearby. So they sacrifice the lamb instead.

2. The man and his wife and children stand anxiously before the priest. They have presented their lamb, so carefully selected that morning from their small flock. The priest lays it on the altar and expertly examines it, running his fingers over its head, looking to see if the

eyes are clear, checking that the limbs are not deformed. Then he looks up and says calmly, 'I find no fault in him.' The family are relieved. The priest takes a sharp knife and slits the animal's throat, deftly catching the spurting blood in a bowl. The father lays the small carcase in a bag, and they take it home to be roasted and eaten with bitter herbs. Another Passover, another lamb.

3. The people are transfixed, also puzzled. In the Temple courtyard, Isaiah stands, prophesying amazing things. Lately, his weighty words have changed from pronouncing judgment over a rebellious nation, to focus on a Person, some kind of future deliverer. The prophecies are rich with metaphors and images of a Servant figure – wise, mighty, strong; yet now a new note of deep sorrow and pain intrudes: 'He was oppressed and afflicted, yet He opened not His mouth. Like a lamb that is led to the slaughter and like a sheep that before His shearers is dumb, so He opened not his mouth ...' The sonorous phrases roll out. The prophet, gripped by powerful emotion, is glimpsing something in the future to which his hearers cannot relate. They look at each other, confused, uncomprehending. Who is this Man, this Lamb?

Session Focus

John 1:29-34

John the Baptist is having wide acclaim and influence. Boldly, he preaches the need for repentance, and announces he is clearing the way for One who is coming, whose sandals he is not worthy to untie.

Then, suddenly, Jesus is walking towards him, and John cries out, 'Look, the Lamb of God, who takes away the sin of the world!' Those standing around are startled. Perhaps some well-taught people recognise the reference to the Lamb: the Passover, the sacrifice, the substitute put to death to atone for sin. The next day the Baptist again identifies Jesus as the Lamb. Something of tremendous significance is dawning on him.

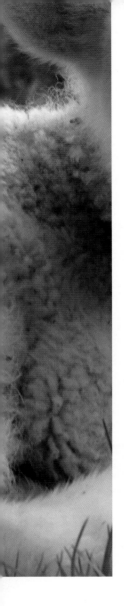

As the Gospel of John unfolds, we see how the Lamb of God walks steadily, faithfully, unflinchingly to the slaughter. John the Baptist fades into the background as Jesus takes centre stage. We watch as He performs miracles which John calls signs, such as: turning gallons of water into wine; healing a paralysed man; restoring sight to a blind man; walking on water; multiplying a small lunch to feed 5,000 people; and raising a dead man to life. We listen as He discourses boldly with Pharisees and lawyers. We see Him abandoning tradition and rigid custom, overthrowing money tables in the Temple, and fearlessly denouncing the Pharisees as whitewashed sepulchres.

Not very lamb-like! More like a roaring lion!

And yet here He is at the well speaking respectfully to a woman despised and outcast because of her immorality; and to another he says, '… neither do I condemn you … Go now and leave your life of sin' (John 8:11). Here He is weeping with His friends outside Lazarus' tomb; and here, He wraps a towel round His waist and washes the disciples' feet. Gentle; humble; compassionate; lamb-like.

Now we see Him, standing before Pilate, clad in a purple robe, which is sticking to the blood congealing on His back, furrowed and gouged from a brutal flogging. A circlet of wicked thorns has been rammed on to His head, and blood pours into His eyes and down His face, sore and raw from where His beard has been tugged out. The crowd is going crazy: 'Crucify Him!' Pilate questions Him, but He gives no answer. 'As a sheep before her shearers is silent …' (Isa. 53:7).

They took Him to the Place of a Skull, and there they crucified Him. The Lamb, bearing away the sin of the world. The weight of guilt, shame, corruption … *our* failure, disobedience, rebellion … these became His. Later Peter would write, 'He himself bore our sins in his body on the tree …' (1 Pet. 2:24).

It was so terrible the disciples didn't understand what was happening.

Later, it all became clear. With dawning joy, they understood. 'Christ, our Passover lamb, has been sacrificed,' Paul wrote to the Corinthians (1 Cor. 5:7), and Peter wrote, '... it was not with perishable things such as silver or gold that you were redeemed ... but with the precious blood of Christ, a lamb without blemish or defect' (1 Pet. 1:18). Like Abraham offering Isaac, the Father of all had sacrificed His only Son, a perfect lamb. But unlike the perpetual sacrifices in the Temple, this was a sacrifice once and for all time, sufficient to remove all guilt from those who believe.

The writer to the Hebrews explained it carefully so that Jews who had been in the system of offering lambs annually, might now realise that 'Christ was sacrificed once to take away the sins of many people' (Heb. 9:28). And not Jews only, but all who believe in Him.

Many years later, John was banished to Patmos Island in the Aegean Sea by a cruel Caesar. There the heavens were opened to him and he had extraordinary visions. A recurring theme was the image of a Lamb standing on the throne bearing dreadful wounds, surrounded by millions of worshipping saints proclaiming, 'Worthy is the Lamb, who was slain, to receive power and wealth and wisdom and strength and honour and glory and praise!' (Rev. 5:12).

The Lamb is now the focus of a great multitude that no one can number, from all tribes, peoples and languages, crying with a loud voice, 'Salvation belongs to our God ... and to the Lamb!' (Rev. 7:10).

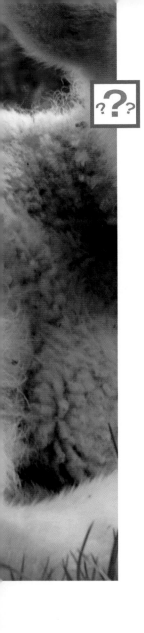

Discussion Starters

1. Read Exodus 12, the institution of the Passover. What is the significance of a lamb 'without defect' (v.5)? What is the significance of the blood on the doorposts (vv.22–28)?

\
\
\
\
\

2. Isaiah 53:6 reminds us that 'We all, like sheep, have gone astray …'. Yet Jesus, the Lamb, did not choose His own way. Matthew 26:36–46 tells how He arrived at the choice He made. Whose will did He choose and why?

\
\
\
\
\

3. We do not employ a sacrificial system any more to purge ourselves from sin, yet we tend to try other methods to make ourselves acceptable. What sort of things might we do? And why is this wrong? It might be helpful to base your thinking on Hebrews 9:12–14.

\
\
\
\
\

4. John wrote three epistles and the Book of Revelation besides his Gospel. 1 John 2:1–2 says: '… we have one who speaks to the Father in our defence – Jesus Christ, the Righteous One. He is the atoning sacrifice for our

sins ...' Looking at the previous chapter, what else does His blood do for us (1 John 1:7–9)?

_____
_____
_____
_____
_____

5. Revelation 12:11 tells us that a potent weapon for the Christian against the accusations of the Enemy is 'the blood of the Lamb'. How do we overcome by the blood of the Lamb?

_____
_____
_____
_____
_____

6. Why do you think Jesus is still depicted as a Lamb in heaven?

_____
_____
_____
_____
_____

7. The moment Jesus died on the cross, the veil in the temple was torn from top to bottom. What relevance does this have to the theme of Jesus as our Lamb?

_____
_____
_____
_____
_____

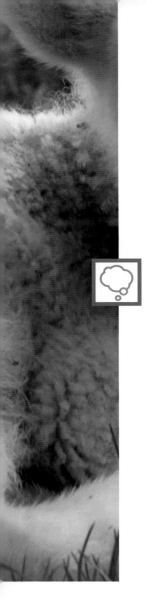

8. 1 Peter 1:18 says 'it was not with ... silver or gold that you were redeemed ... but with the precious blood of Christ, a lamb without blemish ...' Why does Peter use the word 'redeemed' to explain the sacrifice of Jesus?

_____

_____

_____

_____

_____

Final Thoughts

As we have looked at some of the references in the Bible to the Lamb, from Abraham right through to John the Baptist's declaration and on into the Revelation of John, we can see the wonder of God's unfolding plan. Adam's disobedience became embedded in human nature and estranged us from God. But He was determined that sin should be atoned for, and that we human beings should be reconciled to Him. His amazing plan was carefully conceived and meticulously carried out. If Jesus had deviated just once ... had lost His temper, given in to the devil's temptations, had acted independently, had refused to 'drink the cup' ... all would have been lost.

No wonder heaven is alive with worshippers! Let us join them, proclaiming:

All hail the Lamb, enthroned on high
His praise shall be our battle cry.
He reigns victorious, forever glorious,
His name is Jesus, He is the Lord!
Dave Bilbrough, 'All Hail the Lamb'. Copyright ©
Thankyou Music*

... Dear dying Lamb, Thy precious blood
Shall never lose its power
Till all the ransomed Church of God
Be saved, to sin no more.
I do believe, I will believe
That Jesus died for me:
That on the cross He shed His blood
From sin to set me free ...
> William Cowper (1731–1800), from 'There is a
> Fountain Filled with Blood'

Closing Prayer

Lord God, we praise You for the wonder of Jesus laying down His life for us. We praise You that the curtain into the Holy Place was torn apart, symbolising that we may come freely into Your presence. We thank You that Jesus is our sacrifice, the Lamb who has removed our sin, and now we are reconciled to God! Amen.

*See copyright page at front of publication for full copyright notice.

The Resurrection and the Life

John 11:25-44

Icebreaker

Have you ever seen a baby being born? Or a kitten? Maybe a chick hatching? Spring is a time of new life: trees come into leaf, buds appear. Share experiences of seeing new life coming forth.

Opening Prayer

Lord Jesus Christ, we come to You in love and in awe that You have conquered our worst enemy, death. Although we live in frail bodies, we can know the fullness of Your life in us now, and when our bodies come to the end of their usefulness we will leave them behind and enter Your presence, where we can never die. Thank You that You suffered death so that we might move from death into life. Help us to grasp more of the wonder of this truth. Amen.

Bible Readings

Psalm 27:13
I am still confident of this:
I will see the goodness of the LORD
in the land of the living.
Wait for the LORD;
be strong and take heart
and wait for the LORD.

John 1:4
In him was life, and that life was the light of men.

John 11:25
Jesus said to her, 'I am the resurrection and the life. He who believes in me will live, even though he dies; and whoever lives and believes in me will never die. Do you believe this?'

1 John 1:1–4
That which was from the beginning, which we have heard, which we have seen with our eyes, which we have looked at and our hands have touched – this

we proclaim concerning the Word of life. The life appeared; we have seen it and testify to it, and we proclaim to you the eternal life, which was with the Father and has appeared to us. We proclaim to you what we have seen and heard, so that you may have fellowship with us. And our fellowship is with the Father and with his Son, Jesus Christ. We write this to make our joy complete.

Revelation 1:12–18

I turned round to see the voice that was speaking to me. And when I turned I saw seven golden lampstands, and among the lampstands was someone 'like a son of man', dressed in a robe reaching down to his feet and with a golden sash round his chest. His head and hair were white like wool, as white as snow, and his eyes were like blazing fire. His feet were like bronze glowing in a furnace, and his voice was like the sound of rushing waters. In his right hand he held seven stars, and out of his mouth came a sharp double-edged sword. His face was like the sun shining in all its brilliance. When I saw him, I fell at his feet as though dead. Then he placed his right hand on me and said, 'Do not be afraid. I am the First and the Last. I am the Living One; I was dead, and behold I am alive for ever and ever!'

Eye Opener

We now come to Jesus' greatest sign, and the greatest declaration of who He is: the Resurrection and the Life! We have seen that He is water, light, bread, the Lamb, the Shepherd who gives His life; now we come to see that He is Life itself. He created it and He sustains it. Without Him we are subject completely to death, we are without hope. Death is our enemy; Jesus had to confront death and defeat it in order to release us.

Setting the Scene

His pulse was weaker, his breathing shallow, he no longer responded to their voices. Fear clutched at their hearts. The two sisters looked at each other. Yes, they must send for Jesus: it might not be too late! Martha rose and spoke urgently to the young man waiting outside, and he hurried off. She resumed her vigil, crouching by the bed with Mary, stroking her brother's hand. They stayed there until dusk turned to night, and his breathing was no more.

Weeping, they anointed the body, and wrapped it in the grave clothes. A solemn procession accompanying the bier wound its way to the hillside where a cave carved out of the rock gaped open. The corpse was carried in, and a huge circular stone was pushed along a groove until it sealed the entrance. Desolate, the sisters now gave themselves to their overwhelming grief, for four days.

Adding to their misery was a question: why had not Jesus come? He could have come and healed Lazarus! They were such close friends! But He hadn't, and that hurt; it hurt a lot.

Delay is often a hard thing to bear, and difficult for us to understand. For example, why were so many centuries to elapse before the promised Redeemer appeared? Why do some people pray for years for a relative to become a Christian? Why do some struggle so long to be released from a particularly painful circumstance? Our pain clamours for immediate answers!

Yet we see only one side of the story. To Mary and Martha it was hard to understand why Jesus would deliberately stay away from His sick friend, when He alone could have healed him! But Jesus had a greater plan in view, and His plans ripen in His time. He invented time, and His timing is always right. His delays do not contradict His love, as we shall see.

Session Focus

John 11:25–44

On the fourth day, Jesus came. When Martha heard that Jesus was at the outskirts of the village, she hurried to meet Him. In her confusion and grief, she blurted out, 'Lord … if you had been here, my brother would not have died!' (John 11:21). Then, perhaps feeling that she had spoken reproachfully, she added, 'But I know that even now God will give you whatever you ask' (v.22). What did she mean? For sure, she was not expecting a resurrection miracle; but perhaps still looking to Jesus to bring some hope out of the tragedy.

Jesus said, 'Your brother will rise again' (v.23). And then made His astounding assertion: *'I am the resurrection and the life'* (v.25, my emphasis). All through the Gospel, He has offered life: living water, living bread, sight to the blind; now He says 'The life is Me!' He is the embodiment of the promise of life and salvation from God. 'Through him all things were made … In him was life …' (John 1:3).

Could Martha believe that? Can *you* believe that? Perhaps Martha could not fully, but she could affirm her belief that He was the Christ, the Son of God. We shall never, in this life, fully comprehend that He is truly all He says He is. But He requires our simple acceptance that He is the Son of God, and therefore Lord of life and death; Lord of all.

Then Mary came and, falling at His feet, wept with heart-wrenching anguish. Jesus, deeply moved by the sorrow of His friends, wept also. He knew what He was about to do, but it did not prevent Him from feeling their pain. We have a High Priest who sympathises with us (Heb. 4:15). Real tears poured down His face; He felt their sorrow keenly … and I believe He feels ours too.

Yet there was another element to His emotion. The Greek word used, *embrimaomai*, indicates not just sorrow, but anger, indignation. Jesus was witnessing and participating in the ultimate effect of sin on the human

race – the oppression and distress, the misery and finality of death under the tyranny of the devil – and He burned with rage. But Jesus came to destroy him who has the power of death (1 John 3:8), and what happened next was a sign of His authority.

Jesus approached the tomb and ordered the stone to be removed, despite Martha's protest that by now the body would be decomposing. Jesus then prayed so that everyone could hear: 'Father, I thank you that you have heard me' (John 11:41). Remember, He only did what He perceived the Father was doing; He now wanted to make clear that what He was about to do was with the Father's authority. Then He shouted, 'Lazarus, come out!' (v.43). It has been commented that if He had not used Lazarus' name, His shout would have awakened multitudes of dead people!

I wonder what the onlookers expected? A horrible smell pouring out of the darkness, embarrassing and revolting them?

A shrouded figure appeared and shuffled out of the doorway. Lazarus! It is difficult to imagine the effect this must have had on those who watched: shock, fear, astonishment, wonder. Not surprisingly, many believed in Jesus.

This was a real event, but for a moment let us also see that Jesus figuratively wants to roll away stones from people's lives and call life into being out of the hopeless corruption within. People can be scared of having Him call their name because the ugliness of their sin might be exposed. But Jesus comes, not to expose us to humiliation, ridicule and condemnation, but to call us out of rottenness into new clean life!

Mighty as this miracle was, it was but a pale foretaste of what Jesus was to accomplish by His own death and resurrection. Lazarus was brought back to life in his human body, which was destined to die again. Jesus was raised to a new, resurrection body, never to die again. He is the firstborn of a new race, whose human bodies die, but who receive a new eternal life in a resurrection body.

Jesus has defeated our greatest enemy: death. In Him, we also overcome death. It is but a curtain through which we have to pass in order to reach the realm beyond, where all things are made new, and we shall understand what has hitherto been a mystery to us. 'He who believes in me will live, even though he dies; and whoever lives and believes in me will never die' (v.26). This is the heart of the gospel.

Discussion Starters

As we draw towards the end of our Lenten studies, this last discussion section takes on a slightly different form. The first four questions are meant for personal rather than group contemplation. Allow time for quiet reflection before moving on to look at questions 5 to 8 together.

1. Turn to John 20, the wonderful account of the morning of the resurrection. Verses 1–2: let us walk in our imagination with Mary Magdalene to the tomb. What was she feeling as she approached the garden? When she saw the stone rolled away, what did she feel? What did she do?

_____

_____

_____

_____

_____

2. John 20:3–10. Imagine running with Peter and John to the tomb. What did they see? What were their thoughts?

_____

_____

_____

_____

_____

3. John 20:11–18. Mary must have followed Peter and John back into the garden. Linger and meditate on her sorrow, her meeting with the 'gardener' and the wonder in that moment of recognition.

4. Now turn to 1 Corinthians 15:3–10. Note the plain simplicity of this message: Christ died for our sins, was buried, was raised on the third day.

5. 1 Corinthians 15:12–19. Why is our preaching 'useless' if Christ has not been raised?

6. 1 Corinthians 15:20. What does Paul mean by Jesus being the 'firstfruits' of those who have fallen asleep?

7. 1 Corinthians 15:21–26. What does it mean to be 'in Adam' or 'in Christ'? It might be helpful to refer to Romans 5:18–21.

8. John 20:24–29, the story of Thomas at a resurrection appearance of Jesus. Is seeing believing? Compare with 1 Peter 1:8–9. May this be our ongoing experience!

Final Thoughts

Later, it was John who had the revelation of the risen Jesus standing among the lampstands, His eyes like blazing fire, and out of His mouth a two-edged sword, as He exclaimed, 'I am the Living One; I was dead, and behold I am alive for ever and ever! And I hold the keys of death and Hades' (Rev. 1:18). Be comforted: He has the keys! You who are terminally ill, you who have been widowed, you who have suffered grievous bereavement: He has the keys. To you it seemed an accident; or cruel negligence; or just inevitability. We only see our side. He has a bigger plan in view, and greater glory will come out of it. Trust Him, even in the midst of your pain and bewilderment.

Our human bodies will age, die and decay. But those who make Jesus their Lord have the radiant assurance of eternal life begun here and now. Our life-giving

Saviour saves us from present helplessness, hopelessness, emptiness as we embrace His promise of abundant life. Born again, He empowers us to walk as He walked, in peace, love and joyful expectation of glorious new life beyond all that we can ask or think: undeserved, unmerited, unfading, kept in heaven for us!

Let us worship Him.

Closing Prayer

Lord Jesus, my life-giving Saviour, I worship You. One day every knee will bow to You, acknowledging that You are Lord of all. I bow to You now in heartfelt love and thankfulness. I give myself to You, the only reasonable response to the sacrifice that You made for me. Amen.

> ... Lo, Jesus meets us,
> Risen from the tomb!
> Lovingly He greets us,
> Scatters fear and gloom.
> Let the Church with gladness
> Hymns of triumph sing,
> For her Lord now liveth,
> Death has lost its sting.
> *Refrain:*
> *Thine be the glory,*
> *Risen, conquering Son,*
> *Endless is the victory*
> *Thou o'er death hast won!*
>> Edmond Louis Budry (1854–1932), tr. R. Birch Hoyle (1875–1939), from 'Thine be the Glory'

Leader's Notes

Study One: The Water of Life

In advance, look at the Bible passages mentioned in this study. We shall be centring our thinking on John chapter 4, the story of Jesus meeting the Samaritan woman at the well but, before we turn to that, we are going to see that in the Old Testament there was an incident when the Israelites were threatened with dying of thirst in the desert. The story of how Moses struck the rock and water poured out is a prophetic picture which was fulfilled in the New Testament by Jesus.

There are many such events which point forward to something Jesus came to do, and illustrate His life-giving power.

All the images of Jesus in John's Gospel are such 'types'. What is the point of types?

1. They show that God had in mind a plan centuries before Jesus came as a man.

2. They show us that Jesus knew that He had come, not randomly, but was sent by the Father to fulfil the plan.

3. They show us how intricately the Old Testament is bound up with the New; but *especially* how infinitely superior the New Covenant is, which we celebrate in Jesus' death and resurrection.

Before the session starts, have a jug of water and some glasses ready on a table. The icebreaker is about how important water is to our lives; here it is a symbol of the vital necessity of keeping our spirits replenished in the love of God.

Answering the questions could take a lot of time and careful thought. Help the people in your group to apply them. Some may need to think through whether they have ever taken Jesus at His word; some may need to come to Him and drink again. There is no limit; we can come and drink every day!

Study Two: The Bread of Life

If appropriate in your group setting, have bread and wine ready for communion.

This time we shall centre our thoughts on the chapter in John's Gospel where Jesus identifies Himself as the Bread of Life. Again, this echoes an Old Testament incident when Jesus' coming was foreshadowed in Exodus 17 when God sent manna from heaven in answer to the people's demand for bread.

Point out how Jesus Himself resisted the temptation to turn stones into bread and that His spiritual food was to do the will of the Father.

What are we hungry for? How can Jesus satisfy that hunger?

Finish with communion.

Study Three: The Light of the World

The theme of light runs through the Bible. God Himself is light and created light.

John speaks of Jesus as the light not only in the Gospel but in his epistles and in the Book of Revelation. To believe in Jesus and receive Him is to receive spiritual light. John particularly illustrates this by narrating the incident of the healing of the man born blind.

In the Old Testament the nation of Israel is seen as being wilfully blind because they have turned from the light, but any who turn back to God are enlightened again. Isaiah also shows that the light will be made available to people of all races.

Be prepared to pray with any who may feel that there are dark places in their own lives that they need to allow the light of God's truth to shine into and deal with.

Study Four: The Good Shepherd

John chapter 10 is the chapter in which Jesus speaks of Himself as the Shepherd who will lay down His life for the sheep. This leads us to the subject of His death.

However, the discussion questions are based on Psalm 23, which practically everyone is familiar with, but perhaps has not thought about in relation to their own lives. It might also be helpful to look at Jesus' parable of the Lost Sheep in Luke 15.

Help the people in your group to see how they can be shepherded by Jesus. This isn't just a nice 'soft' idea; it is actually about down-to-earth issues concerning dangers we might encounter; how the shepherd may help us make choices; and how He may train and discipline us. It is also about being part of a flock. What benefits are there in being in a 'flock', ie the Church, the people of God?

Study Five: The Lamb of God

We come now to see how Jesus was the fulfilment of the whole sacrificial system introduced by Moses in the Old Testament. And how important it is to see the historical roots of what He did on the cross. He was the Lamb led to the slaughter, whom Isaiah prophesied, and He makes sense of all those enigmatic allusions.

Begin with the story of Abraham and Isaac, as it so poignantly and beautifully illustrates for us the huge cost of God's demand that the Son, the promised One, be slain. We also witness Abraham's obedience and the substitution of the lamb when Isaac is reprieved.

The theme continues through to the final chapter of the Bible: a Lamb is on the throne.

It would be good to celebrate communion at the end, if appropriate in your group setting.

Study Six: The Resurrection and the Life

The culmination of John's Gospel story is, of course, Jesus' death and resurrection; but it is the beginning of new life for those who put their trust in Him.

This might be a great opportunity to help any in need of assurance of their salvation to be affirmed in their faith.

It might also be a time of comforting any facing death or who have been recently bereaved, as we contemplate the glorious truth of the hope we have of resurrection life because of what Jesus has accomplished for us.

It would be good to finish with a time of communion and thanksgiving.

National Distributors

UK: (and countries not listed below)
CWR, Waverley Abbey House, Waverley Lane, Farnham, Surrey GU9 8EP.
Tel: (01252) 784700 Outside UK (44) 1252 784700 Email: mail@cwr.org.uk

AUSTRALIA: KI Entertainment, Unit 21 317-321 Woodpark Road, Smithfield, New South Wales 2164.
Tel: 1 800 850 777 Fax: 02 9604 3699 Email: sales@kientertainment.com.au

CANADA: David C Cook Distribution Canada, PO Box 98, 55 Woodslee Avenue, Paris,
Ontario N3L 3E5. Tel: 1800 263 2664 Email: sandi.swanson@davidccook.ca

GHANA: Challenge Enterprises of Ghana, PO Box 5723, Accra. Tel: (021) 222437/223249
Fax: (021) 226227 Email: ceg@africaonline.com.gh

HONG KONG: Cross Communications Ltd, 1/F, 562A Nathan Road, Kowloon.
Tel: 2780 1188 Fax: 2770 6229 Email: cross@crosshk.com

INDIA: Crystal Communications, 10-3-18/4/1, East Marredpalli, Secunderabad – 500026, Andhra Pradesh.
Tel/Fax: (040) 27737145 Email: crystal_edwj@rediffmail.com

KENYA: Keswick Books and Gifts Ltd, PO Box 10242-00400, Nairobi.
Tel: (254) 20 312639/3870125 Email: keswick@swiftkenya.com

MALAYSIA: Canaanland, No. 25 Jalan PJU 1A/41B, NZX Commercial Centre, Ara Jaya, 47301 Petaling Jaya,
Selangor. Tel: (03) 7885 0540/1/2 Fax: (03) 7885 0545 Email: info@canaanland.com.my

Salvation Book Centre (M) Sdn Bhd, 23 Jalan SS 2/64, 47300 Petaling Jaya, Selangor.
Tel: (03) 78766411/78766797 Fax: (03) 78757066/78756360
Email: info@salvationbookcentre.com

NEW ZEALAND: KI Entertainment, Unit 21 317-321 Woodpark Road, Smithfield,
New South Wales 2164, Australia. Tel: 0 800 850 777 Fax: +612 9604 3699
Email: sales@kientertainment.com.au

NIGERIA: FBFM, Helen Baugh House, 96 St Finbarr's College Road, Akoka, Lagos.
Tel: (01) 7747429/4700218/825775/827264 Email: fbfm_1@yahoo.com

PHILIPPINES: OMF Literature Inc, 776 Boni Avenue, Mandaluyong City.
Tel: (02) 531 2183 Fax: (02) 531 1960 Email: gloadlaon@omflit.com

SINGAPORE: Alby Commercial Enterprises Pte Ltd, 95 Kallang Avenue #04-00, AIS Industrial Building, 339420.
Tel: (65) 629 27238 Fax: (65) 629 27235 Email: marketing@alby.com.sg

SOUTH AFRICA: Struik Christian Books, 80 MacKenzie Street, PO Box 1144, Cape Town 8000.
Tel: (021) 462 4360 Fax: (021) 461 3612 Email: info@struikchristianmedia.co.za

SRI LANKA: Christombu Publications (Pvt) Ltd, Bartleet House, 65 Braybrooke Place, Colombo 2.
Tel: (9411) 2421073/2447665 Email: dhanad@bartleet.com

USA: David C Cook Distribution Canada, PO Box 98, 55 Woodslee Avenue, Paris, Ontario N3L 3E5, Canada.
Tel: 1800 263 2664 Email: sandi.swanson@davidccook.ca

CWR is a Registered Charity - Number 294387
CWR is a Limited Company registered in England - Registration Number 1990308

Courses and seminars

Publishing and new media

Conference facilities

Transforming lives

CWR's vision is to enable people to experience personal transformation through applying God's Word to their lives and relationships.

Our Bible-based training and resources help people around the world to:
• Grow in their walk with God
• Understand and apply Scripture to their lives
• Resource themselves and their church
• Develop pastoral care and counselling skills
• Train for leadership
• Strengthen relationships, marriage and family life and much more.

Our insightful writers provide daily Bible-reading notes and other resources for all ages, and our experienced course designers and presenters have gained an international reputation for excellence and effectiveness.

CWR's Training and Conference Centre in Surrey, England, provides excellent facilities in an idyllic setting – ideal for both learning and spiritual refreshment.

CWR, Waverley Abbey House,
Waverley Lane, Farnham,
Surrey GU9 8EP, UK

Telephone: +44 (0)1252 784700
Email: info@cwr.org.uk
Website: www.cwr.org.uk

Registered Charity No 294387
Company Registration No 1990308

Apply deeper biblical understanding to your life each day

These popular daily Bible-reading notes will provide you with in-depth and relevant study of the Bible. Each bimonthly issue includes contributions from two different authors and covers an Old Testament book, a New Testament book – and you'll explore a psalm for each weekend.

Over a five-year period, you will be taken through the entire Bible. Get started today!

Cover to Cover Every Day
by various well-known writers
64-page booklets, 120x170mm

For current prices visit www.cwr.org.uk/store
Available online or from Christian bookshops.

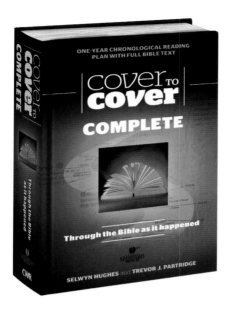

Take an amazing journey of discovery

Reading the whole Bible in the order events happened is one of the most exciting and rewarding journeys you could take.

And CWR's award-winning *Cover to Cover Complete* makes the journey highly engaging and spiritually nourishing with:

- The *Holman Christian Standard* translation arranged in chronological order
- Beautiful charts, maps, illustrations and diagrams
- Timelines to track the context of each day's reading
- Devotional thoughts that make each passage relevant to your life
- Additional information and illustrations on CWR's website.

Why not get your church or small group to read *Cover to Cover Complete* together? Special bulk prices are available and we'll give you your own online forum to share your discoveries with each other. To find out more visit **www.cwr.org.uk/journey**

Re-thinki
Worshiρ.

Jan Berry

St Marks CRC Press Sheffield

Together in Hope
Resources for Christian Faith Today

This series of resource books results from a number of organisations
working together to give encouragement
and hope to those who seek a credible Christian faith
for the twenty-first century.

We hope that these books will be helpful to those individuals
and groups, inside and outside of the Church, who are
exploring matters of faith and belief.

We are grateful to our authors and encourage others
to offer their services.

For further information about the sponsoring
organisations please see the back cover. If you wish to
contact the editorial group, please email:
togetherinhope.editor@gmail.com

The current convenor is Adrian Alker

The books in this series can be bought via the PCN Britain and Modern
Church websites (see back cover) or telephone 0114 274 6266

Printed on recycled paper by Pickards.org.uk Sheffield S2 4BB

Foreword

For many who seek a credible Christian faith in this twenty-first century, participation in public worship can raise challenging questions about the nature of God, the use of language and the very practice and purpose of such acts of worship.

Much has been written about prayer and liturgy over the centuries and numerous resources are available to those involved in planning and leading worship. Yet the difficult issues about language and meaning remain an obstacle for many who might wish to be part of a worshipping community.

In this booklet Jan Berry addresses these issues in a gentle and yet comprehensive rethink about Christian worship. Throughout Jan offers ways in which worship can help us to connect with our sense of transcendence and the world around us. For many in the churches, this booklet will hopefully encourage discussion about the ways in which their offering of worship can speak, with integrity, to modern day believers. For others, the issues and suggestions made here might offer ways in which those who question, search and yearn for authentic spiritual experiences can indeed discover them, in part, within an act of worship.

We are grateful to Jan Berry who has brought her considerable knowledge and experience as a pastor, liturgist and teacher to add to the books in this Together In Hope series.

Adrian Alker

Jan Berry

Jan Berry is a minister of the United Reformed Church working in theological education at Luther King House in Manchester. She teaches various aspects of practical theology, including liturgy and worship, and has a particular interest in feminist liturgy and spirituality. She has written and published prayers and hymns for use in worship, and is keen to encourage others in the process of creating liturgy.

Re-thinking Worship?

Contents

1. Introduction

Ask any group of Christians to describe an experience of worship, and you will get a variety of answers. For one person it is the sense of transcendence and mystery in Orthodox liturgy, for another the immediacy and spontaneity of a Pentecostal service. One person will encounter God in the messy playfulness of all-age worship, whilst another will be uplifted by the formality and structure of a sung Eucharist. For some, repeated words and a formal liturgy are 'vain repetition'; for others an informal sharing of bread and wine in groups on the grass in the open is casual and irreverent. And for some, worship is the private sense of prayerfulness of a walk in the mountains, or listening to music in the comfort of their home.

However we understand it, worship has been seen as an essential part of Christian life and discipleship, and corporate worship as the foundation of the church's life. Whatever other activities and programmes make up the life of a congregation, at some point there is usually a gathering which includes prayer and praise, the expounding of Scripture, and the celebration of Eucharist.

Yet for many progressive Christians, the regular worship and liturgy of the church can be problematic in a number of ways.

All too often, the familiar words and imagery raise intellectual questions that remain unanswered. Whilst in our thinking we have left behind the idea of a God 'up there', or miraculous answers to prayer, or manifestations of the supernatural, in worship we find ourselves using words and images that are rooted in a world where we no longer feel at home. Worship seems to invite us to participate in a form of intellectual dishonesty, in which we cannot engage with integrity.

For many people, such as women, people with disabilities, lesbians, gay men and trans people, or people of colour, the primary feeling of worship may be one of exclusion. Women have drawn attention to the exclusive language of 'mankind', 'brotherhood', 'sonship', and the dominance of male imagery for God. Others have challenged the use of language of disability, or of blackness or darkness in negative senses; and often those who are single or in relationships other than heterosexual marriage feel that their experience is invisible and marginalised by the dominance of heterosexual or family images.

Finally, worship that stresses our weaknesses and helplessness before an almighty God can leave us with feelings of guilt and dependency – that somehow we have not done or said all that we should, and that we are worthless, miserable creatures. Rather than leaving us feeling uplifted and encouraged, all too often worship can leave us feeling unheard, our needs unmet, and our sense of self-worth damaged. Sometimes worship should carry a spiritual health warning!

Yet worship should not, and need not, be like this. Worship can inspire us with a sense of the mystery and wonder of the divine, taking us beyond ourselves into a place of beauty and awe. Worship can help to create a sense of belonging and community, strengthening the ties of relationship. Worship can build up our faith, stretching our understanding, and challenging and inspiring us to fresh commitment.

In this booklet let us reflect on what we mean by worship, particularly in relation to the corporate worship and liturgy of the church. We will look at some of the elements of worship, such as space and symbol, language and imagery, to see how they might become more effective in helping us to encounter a sense of the divine and build community. We will explore what it means to share bread and wine in the sacrament of Eucharist, or Communion. Finally we will look at the possibilities for change, and how we might go about exploring the potential for transforming worship in our own contexts.

Each chapter will end with some questions for discussion or reflection, and a suggestion for worship and prayer. These can be used by individuals, or shared within a group. At the end of the booklet you will find suggestions for further reading, and a list of resources that could be used in worship.

What do we mean by worship?

Just as there are many different experiences of worship, so there are many different definitions or ways of understanding what is going on. In this chapter we look at and critique different ways of understanding worship, seeing their strengths and their limitations, and trying to find a way of expressing the purpose and intention of worship that can be helpful to progressive Christians.

We begin by looking at some of the traditional definitions of worship and liturgy, and how they might help or hinder us in understanding what people are doing when they gather for worship.

One of the traditional understandings of the word 'worship' is derived from 'worth-ship'; it is about acknowledging the worth of God. In this understanding, worship is about recognising the glory and the majesty of a divine being, transcendent and far above us. For many people, this in itself is problematic, and not consistent with the idea of a God who is immanent, alongside and within us, a presence or energy in the world. We need a way of finding meaning in worship which is intellectually congruent with our beliefs.

Another commonly used word is 'liturgy', often used to refer to a set and prescribed form of worship. It is actually derived from two Greek words, 'laos' and 'ergos', and literally means 'the work of the people'. In Paul's use of the word in Romans 12:1 it refers to the whole of our Christian living, which should be our 'work' offered to God. Often however, it seems that worship is removed from the needs, emotions and daily lives of the people in the pews. If our corporate worship is truly to be 'the work of the people' then there needs to be a coherence and connection between what we do and say in church, and the whole of our faithful living and believing.

Worship: honouring God's worth?

One common way of looking at worship is that it is the duty and obligation of humanity; it is what we owe to the God who has created and redeemed us. In this understanding, worship does not have to be relevant or inspiring. It does not matter what we feel, because our worship is what is due to God.

However, there are difficulties with this understanding of worship. It implies a hierarchical and anthropomorphic view of God: a divine being, far removed from us, who demands homage and adoration. In the women's spirituality group I attend, some are reluctant to use the word 'worship' at all, as it carries so much of this kind of resonance. If we are questioning the existence of a God 'out there', and instead focusing, as the Quakers do, on the sense of a divine spirit or light within humanity, then this definition of worship as homage to an external, superior, transcendent being will have little meaning for us. If it is difficult for us to think of, or image, God in anthropomorphic terms then to think of worship in this way will feel dishonest, and lacking in integrity.

For some people there is a strength in this understanding of worship. For those who belong to a tradition which uses a fixed and constantly-repeated liturgy, there can be a sense of being carried by the familiar words and phrases at times when faith seems low or absent, and prayer difficult or impossible. I remember, as a Baptist student, occasionally attending an Orthodox church. On one occasion a member of the congregation said to us: 'In your tradition, the service can be a success or a failure, depending on the preacher; with us, the liturgy just happens, it just is'. Whilst it may seem to some to be a dishonest restriction, the sense of a liturgy that 'just is' and that does not depend on our feelings and state of mind may offer a secure framework to others.

Worship: nurturing the believer?

Another way of looking at worship is more subjective, placing an emphasis on its value for the worshipper. Worship is about strengthening and nurturing faith, about building relationships and community with other believers, so that we go out feeling inspired and challenged for our daily living. This, I suspect, is what people mean when they talk about worship 'charging the batteries'! In this model, worship is primarily about what happens internally for the believer: it is an attitude of mind and heart. If worship is not inspirational, then either this is a failing on the part of the Christian worshipper, or it means the worship is somehow not spiritual, but empty and mechanical. In this understanding of worship, it is important that the worship is relevant for those who are there, meaningful and accessible to them.

I suspect that many would have sympathy with this perspective, in that we hope to find worship helpful or meaningful in some way. However, to view worship solely in this way makes it dependent on the person leading or planning the worship, or on the elements within it which appeal to particular individuals. It is very subjective, and can lead almost to a consumer attitude to worship, with people shopping around to find church communities and congregations where the worship is congenial to them.

Each of these understandings of worship has something in its favour. There are times when the corporate liturgy of the church can carry us through times of doubt and difficulty, when 'going through the motions' is all that is possible for us; and we are held by the worship and prayer of the community of faith. Equally there are times when we find inspiration, comfort or challenge in the words of a prayer, or in the familiarity of a well-loved hymn. But both have their weaknesses too, and raise questions for us about whether we can actually participate in worship with integrity.

Worship as connection

I would like to propose another way of looking at worship, which is about connection. In this way of looking at it, worship becomes about helping us to feel a sense of connection - at a number of different levels. First of all, worship should help us connect with whatever we understand of the divine. Whether we believe in a transcendent deity, who is beyond our understanding and comprehension, or whether we affirm that sense of the divine within everyone, worship and prayer at its best will help us discover that sense of mystery and presence. Secondly, worship should help us connect with what is going on within ourselves: it needs to speak to our hopes and fears, our dreams and anxieties, our longings for a better life and a more just world. And thirdly, such worship should not remain inward looking, but should also help to strengthen and nurture our sense of connection with the world around us, both in terms of our immediate relationships, and the social and global issues which confront us.

This sense of connection is constantly there; it is like breathing, part of our living and existing in the world. But like breathing, there are times when it is particularly helpful to be aware of it. Worship and prayer are about cultivating and focusing on that sense of connection which undergirds our lived faith.

The relationship of worship and belief

Underlying this discussion of worship is another fundamental issue about the relationship between worship and belief.

The phrase 'lex orandi, lex credendi' - as we pray, so we believe (literally, 'the law of praying, the law of believing') - dates back to the patristic period and has been used in liturgical scholarship to denote the way in which theology influences and affects our faith. In other words, what people say, sing and do in worship will affect and shape their theology; and I would argue that when words are wedded to ritual action or to music, their effect is even more profound, working at a level that is deeper than the conscious cerebral understanding.

The use of this phrase for the relation of theology to worship can be interpreted in two ways.

Traditionally, it has been understood to mean that liturgical texts must be closely scrutinized for their adherence to correct or sound doctrine. Often texts are produced by liturgical commissions and approved by ecclesial authority before they are issued for regular use by congregations. In traditions which do not use set texts there are often unwritten rules and norms about what is acceptable theologically in worship; for example, attempts to change the dominance of male language and imagery for God meet resistance on the grounds that this is theologically wrong or even heresy. In this understanding of 'lex orandi, lex credendi', it is restrictive; it is a way of ensuring that correct, or approved or authorized theological concepts are enshrined in the liturgy in such a way that they become embedded in the minds and hearts of worshippers.

But there is another more dynamic way of interpreting 'lex orandi, lex credendi'. In this understanding, liturgy is an active process of shaping theology. Rather than a vehicle for conveying received texts or norms, liturgy is seen as engaging with scripture and the human story, with sacrament and experience, in an interactive and dynamic process of negotiation. Alternative forms of worship and liturgy emerging in the late twentieth and early twenty-first centuries are constructing and shaping theology for a post-modern generation. In some instances this may be a conscious and intentional process, in others it may be a half-realised search for words and images that make sense of Gospel story and divine activity for a particular context or congregation. Either way, the theology is not pre-formed and handed down, but is emerging from the experience of searching for God in new ways of worship and prayer. Our worship therefore becomes a way of 'doing theology'. New concepts and images of God, new ways of speaking about the life and work of Jesus, new understandings of the Spirit's working amongst us, emerge in the process of transforming and constructing liturgy. In this way liturgy really can become 'the work of the people', as we engage in the dynamic creative process of constructing theology.

Conclusion

No one way of thinking about worship will speak to each individual's need. Some will want to stress the objective nature of worship, but seek to find ways in which they can express honour to God without compromising their questions and beliefs. Others will want to emphasize worship as the source of inspiration and challenge, affirming the individual and creating community. For some, seeking a sense of connection with the depths of themselves and the world around them will foster a sense of connection with the divine.

But for all of us, worship has the potential to shape our theology; if we can engage in it with a playful and creative spirit, it can be transformative.

Questions for discussion/reflection

1. Think of a recent experience of worship, whatever that term means to you! What was positive and helpful about it, or what was negative?

2. Which of the understandings of worship described above do you find helpful, and why?

3. How does your usual practice of worship (if you have one) relate to the beliefs you hold? Can you think of any ways in which worship has helped to shape your belief?

A suggestion for worship or prayer

Take some time to think about what gives you a sense of the divine: relationships, music, art, nature. Find moments when you can pause to focus on that, developing your awareness and strengthening the sense of connectedness.

2. Space and Symbol

I was brought up in a tradition that always stressed, 'The church is the people, not the building'. The words 'For where two or three are gathered in my name, I am there amongst them' (Matt 18:20) were often used to remind us that location and numbers were not important, and that God's people could gather together to worship anywhere, at any time.

And yet I have become increasingly aware of the importance of space. If we take seriously the idea of incarnation, of the Word made flesh, then we must see our bodies and our senses as holy; they are part of the flesh that God in Christ takes on. Incarnation is not a once-and-for-all, unique event, but a story and an image of the way God dwells with us in our embodied world.

Sacred space

The concept of 'sacred space' is an ancient and enduring one. In the Old Testament we find sacred stones put up to mark encounters with God, the sense of God's presence in the Ark, and then in the Temple. Other religions have their sacred places and temples, and stone circles and monuments such as Stonehenge speak of the sense of the sacred in cultic ritual. In the early days of Christianity we find a separation from temple and synagogue as people gathered for worship in homes. But by the third century Christians were beginning to construct buildings specifically for the purpose of worship. When Christianity became recognised by the Roman Empire, these buildings began to take the form of the Roman basilica, with its nave and aisles, with its raised dais for the priest, assuming the position of power as the Roman magistrate had done. Such architecture still determines the form and shape of many of our church buildings today.

However, the concept of 'sacred space' goes beyond buildings. For some, buildings are important; the architecture and art of a great Cathedral can speak of the majesty and greatness of God. Others will find more of a sense of divine presence in nature: on the mountain tops, or by a still lake, or experiencing the constant movement of waves crashing on a shore.

When I visited Israel/Palestine, we were taken to many of the sacred sites in Jerusalem and Bethlehem. I found myself unmoved by the crowds in the Church of the Holy Sepulchre, or by the silver star marking the (supposed) place of Jesus' birth. But walking down the Mount of Olives, and looking out of the window of the tiny 'Dominus Flevit' (The Lord wept) chapel over Jerusalem, I could imagine Jesus weeping over this divided city. Walking down the Mount of Beatitudes and by the shore of Lake Galilee helped me recall the familiar stories, and brought them to life in my imagination.

So what makes space 'sacred' for us? Sometimes it is the beauty - of a landscape, or a building - that inspires a sense of awe and wonder, of transcendence, helping us to catch a glimpse of something beyond ourselves that we may choose to name as divine. Sometimes it is the memories or associations that the place holds for us: the memory of a significant occasion or moment in our own personal journey. Sometimes it is because a place has been a place of prayer and pilgrimage for generations, so that the very air seems to resonate with the faith of people who have gone before. Sometimes it is the quiet and peacefulness that allows us to retreat, to draw away from the noise and bustle and the constant demands of everyday life.

The word 'sacred' carries with it the notion of something set apart, holy in a way that is different from the mundane experience of our everyday living. However, there is a difficulty with this; surely God or the divine is in every place, and part of our day-to-day living? There seems to be a tension between a belief in an omnipresent God or divine spirit, and the notion of special places, set apart and in some way special or different. But as human beings, perhaps we need that focusing of God's presence in particular times or places. Just as a piece of glass can focus and concentrate the sun's light, so the divine light within becomes focused in places that move or inspire us, or have been intentionally designated as places of worship and prayer. They do not guarantee God's presence but they offer that opportunity for encounter, of stripping away the barriers and the distractions, so that we can make that connection with what is at the root and ground of our very being. Of course we can encounter God in the midst of a crowded city or a derelict street; but there are places that are, in the words of George Macleod in describing Iona, 'thin' places, where the separation between earth and heaven seems less, and we experience a sense of the transcendent.

Symbol and symbolic action

Just as some places take on something of the sacred, so the way they are laid out, and the symbols and the images that are used, can help to convey a sense of the sacred. The structure and architecture of our buildings can speak of our concept of God; the magnificence or height or grandeur of a building may reflect a concept of a powerful, hierarchical God. Traditionally, many church buildings have been designed in such a way that they seem to point upwards: a spire or a steeple pointing to the heavens, an aisle leading up to the altar. But writers such as Lesley Northup, (Northup, 1997) in writing of women's ritual, talks of the distinction between vertical and horizontal space; the vertical is linked with understandings of a superior, hierarchical Being, whereas horizontal space stresses relationships with others in worship. So the way the building is laid out and the way we use the space have their effect on the way we understand God and the divine/human relationship.

The symbols that we use in worship are important too. We have the traditional symbols of water, bread and wine, the altar or the Communion table, the pulpit or the lectern, liturgical colours representing the Christian year used for altar cloths or vestments. But increasingly other symbols are being used in contemporary worship. The traditional practice of lighting candles is an ancient one in many traditions, but now increasingly common in those churches formerly suspicious of symbols; there is a common use of stones or shells or a variety of other objects to symbolise our prayers; and projected images onto a screen, and the use of banners or coloured cloths to symbolise the seasons of the year have become features of worship in many places.

Symbols are important to us because they work at many levels. They appeal to our senses - of sight or sound or smell - and take us beyond forms of worship that are purely cerebral or verbal. A symbol can convey powerfully an idea which would take many words to explain. It can mean different things to different people. However, there is a risk to this too; people may not understand the symbol in the way that is intended. Symbols that have been used for many years can be powerful because of their memories or associations; but they can also become obsolete, so unfamiliar that their meaning is lost unless it is explained, or so familiar that they lose their power to communicate.

A symbol can also be used as a focus for silence or contemplation. We may hold a stone in our hands, marvelling at the way it has been formed over centuries, or watch the flickering flame of a candle. Our senses of touch and sight come into play, to help us focus our mental and spiritual energy, concentrating it and just 'being' in the moment.

The symbol 'participates in that to which it points' (Tillich, 1957). Whilst the candle is not literally the light of Christ, it participates in that light and conveys it to us. When we talk lightly of something being 'just symbolic', we are disregarding the power of the symbol to help us make that connection with our sense of the divine. This means that our symbols need to be congruent; there needs to be a connection, that we can recognise and affirm, between the symbolic object and the meaning it is hoped to convey.

Symbolic action is also a powerful vehicle for our worship. Many of us can remember being told to 'close your eyes and put your hands together' for prayer. This may have come to seem an empty formality, but nevertheless taking up a bodily posture is a ritual action that can bring about the emotion or state of mind we are wishing to enter. So kneeling may suggest devotion, respect, and obedience; or it may have uncomfortable connotations of submission and subjection. Opening our hands for prayer, or standing with upraised arms for praise, will be helpful to some. Ritual, and symbolic action, is performative: in doing an action, we are participating in bringing about a desired result.

In our worship the creative arts can work in similar ways to enhance our experience of connectedness with another realm. Art (whether painting, banners, sculpture or installation) appeals to the visual, and can take us beyond ourselves. Movement, dance and drama can be used to portray meaning in embodied form. Music can lift us beyond the immediate moment and comfort, inspire or challenge us, evoking powerful feelings and memories. In the past the use of the creative arts required skills and resources not available in many congregations, but modern technology has opened up a range of different possibilities and resources to enrich our worship.

Conclusion

Sacred space, symbols and symbolic action - all point to the reality that our worship is embodied. We may seek to worship 'in spirit and in truth' (John 4:24) but we are physical, embodied human beings, and the worship or prayer of our spirits is expressed and to a certain extent shaped by what we do with our bodies. Finding a place that helps us feel a sense of connection, using symbols and symbolic action to help us sense the divine, is an embodiment of our worship.

Ideas for discussion/reflection

1. Focus on a place that is special, or sacred, for you. What makes it so? Is that sense of sacredness, or specialness, something that can help you in your worship?

2. If you are meeting regularly as a group, suggest the week before that everyone brings an object which has symbolic value for them. Share these objects and their stories in the group; then discuss what symbols or symbolic action you find helpful in worship.

Suggestion for worship or prayer

If you are on your own, spend some time in silence, focusing on a candle or a cross, or a natural object. In a group, invite people to light candles, or place stones or shells in a bowl, as a sign of their own prayers.

3. The Language of Worship

Whilst our surroundings in worship, and the visual images and symbols we use are important, most forms of worship (with the possible exception of Quaker meetings) depend in part on words. The language we use to convey our prayers and praise, or to seek to understand the Scriptures, is a vital element in our liturgy. In this chapter we explore the ways in which we use words in worship, in our prayers, hymns, readings and expounding of Scripture.

Language as metaphor

I begin by arguing that no language can do justice to God. There is a sense in which God is unknowable, uncontainable in human words and language. Whether we think of God as transcendent Spirit, or the mystery at the depths of our being, we are talking of something that is beyond our grasp. The apophatic tradition in prayer and spirituality stresses the impossibility of finding adequate language for God; all our language is limited, and we can only describe what God is not, or refrain from language altogether and fall into silence. Whilst in the mystic tradition this has been a helpful way into prayer for many, in most of our worship we tend to use words. It is important therefore that we remember the limits of language; the language of worship is metaphorical and poetic. Metaphor indicates something of the reality we are pointing to, without describing it wholly. When we talk of life as a journey, we are not talking about literal movement through space; we are using a metaphor. When we speak of the church as a family, we do not literally mean that people in the church are biologically related; we are using a metaphor to convey the idea that a church has some of the characteristics of a family. When we talk of God as rock, or light, or living water, we are not talking literally; we are using metaphor. God is not a rock, or light or water, but these words help us to understand something of what God is like. Some metaphors have become so familiar that we no longer recognise them as such, and this has happened with the well-used term of 'Father' for God. This is a metaphor; God is not literally a father in the biological sense, but has some of the characteristics that we associate with fatherhood. To take our metaphorical language literally is a form of idolatry.

Because our metaphors are partial and incomplete, using as many different metaphors as possible can enrich our worship. This is what the Psalmists do. Read through the psalms and you will find a huge range of similes and metaphors for addressing God. There are the familiar ones, such as 'King' and 'Shepherd'; there are also 'Rock', 'Fortress', 'Shield', 'Shadow of Wings', 'Light', 'Refuge', 'Mother's Breast', and many more! By piling up metaphors, being creative and playful, we can enrich our worship and expand our consciousness and awareness of who or what the Divine is.

Inclusive language

But we need to look carefully at the metaphors we use, to ensure that they are fully inclusive and relevant.

The importance of inclusive language was first raised by Christian feminists, who drew attention to the dominance of male language and imagery in our worship (reflecting a much wider male dominance in the leadership and hierarchy of the churches). Feminist theology draws attention to the fact that using male language of worshippers is exclusive of women; we are not sons or brothers, and do not feel part of 'mankind'. For some this is simply dismissed as 'political correctness', but for many it is an issue of social justice, and stems from a genuine desire to create a sense of welcome and inclusion in worship.

If we accept that all of us are made in God's image, then our language for the divine needs to reflect that too. For centuries, our language of the divine has been dominated by male terminology - Father, King, Lord - which does not enable women to see themselves reflected in the divine. Some would argue therefore for gender-neutral terms: God as Friend, or Creator, or Shepherd, for example. The problem with this is that such is the dominance of male imagery for God, it is likely to be heard as male. As one person remarked to me in a seminar, 'Surely God doesn't have a gender. He's neither male nor female, is he?' So we need to balance the male imagery with female imagery, of God as mother, giving birth, as old woman, as Wisdom/Sophia. Sometimes we may want to use words that are linked to activities often done by women – God as weaver, bread maker and so on, although there is a danger that this could lead to a reinforcing of female stereotypes. Some would prefer to avoid personal imagery for the divine altogether, arguing that it leads to an anthropomorphic concept of God which is inappropriate or unhelpful. But so long as we remember all our imagery - personal or impersonal - is metaphorical, using a whole range of metaphors and images may open up new ways of seeing and describing the invisible, indescribable mystery.

Whilst an awareness of inclusive language may begin with gender, there are other ways in which language can be exclusive. Much of our traditional language and imagery associates white and light with goodness and purity, whilst blackness and darkness are used to suggest evil and sin. For many people, this is offensive and perpetuates a kind of implicit racism. Others have drawn attention to the way in which we use the language of disability so that we are 'blind' to God's love, 'deaf' to God's word, 'paralysed' by sin. Words which are used to describe disability thus become associated with sin and weakness, perpetuating negative connotations of disability and leaving people feeling excluded and alienated.

Other metaphors can cause difficulty because they are militaristic or hierarchical. The language and imagery of kingship, of the Lord of Hosts, of battle and war, have their roots in a picture of God which is contrary to what we see in the Gospel stories of Jesus. Here Jesus comes as one who is alongside the marginalised and oppressed, meeting and eating with the poor and the excluded. Triumphalist language reinforces our social power relations and dynamics; language of victory and overcoming may be appropriate when it expresses the longings of the oppressed, but not when it perpetuates the power and might of those who are dominant or privileged.

Our language is metaphorical, but metaphors can lose their power when they are overused or become obsolete over time. We need to explore ways of creating new metaphors and imagery which are relevant and accessible for the context of our contemporary worship. Imagery of God as shepherd would have meant a lot to people in biblical times, for whom shepherding was a part of daily life; it may have less resonance for contemporary urban Christians. If our worship is to come alive, and be truly accessible and contextual, it needs to reflect the realities of life in a post-modern, technologically developed society.

The form and shape of prayer

A large part of any service of corporate worship is likely to take the form of prayer, which will vary according to the tradition and practice of the church and/or its denomination. Some will be determined by a fixed liturgy; some will use prayers written or chosen from published collections for that particular service, and some will use extemporary prayer. Most prayers will be verbal, but we may also use pictures, images or icons to help us to pray. Whatever our practice, there are a number of elements of prayer which are likely to be present in most services.

There will be prayers of praise, adoration and thanksgiving. These may focus on God's acts in creation, God's saving activity in Christ and in the world, and the blessings of God experienced in everyday living and relationship. For many of us, the idea of adoration of a superior being is difficult; but a sense of wonder and mystery at the universe around us, or of appreciation and thankfulness for moments of joy or gift that we have experienced may help us to capture something of that sense of praise.

Prayers of confession can easily concentrate on our worthlessness and humility before God, leaving us feeling defeated and inadequate. Perhaps it is more helpful to focus on injustice and inequality in the world, recognising our privilege, and the demands of God upon our lives.

Prayers of intercession can be particularly difficult. They suggest an interventionist God who needs to be persuaded to act. Many prayers of intercession avoid this by simply asking for an increase in our own awareness and willingness to act; but there is also a power in simply holding situations and people in the sense of God's love, seeking to make a connection with the God who suffers with and in the world.

The power of hymns

St. Augustine is reputed to have said, 'He who sings prays twice', and there is certainly a power in singing hymns that goes beyond the power of words alone.

At a workshop for a project on hymnody, I tried to demonstrate how hymns stick in our minds by asking the group to sing (without any copies of the words) the first verse of 'There is a green hill far away'; they went on to sing the whole of the hymn! Now I am sure there were many of us in that group who would be ill at ease with the theory of substitutionary atonement implicit in that hymn, yet, like it or not, those words were embedded in our consciousness from our childhood Sunday school days.

I think there are a number of reasons why hymns remain in our minds in that way.

Firstly, hymns have memories and associations for us. For many people, a particular hymn is significant because it was sung at their wedding or at a family funeral. Some hymns take us back to particular occasions in our lives, and regardless of the actual words or theology, they recall the emotions and significance of that time.

Secondly, hymns use rhyme and rhythm to make them memorable. Some, such as modern worship songs or choruses, or Taizé chants, also use repetition. The metric structure and the rhyme scheme, although we may not be consciously aware of them as we are singing, help the words to become embedded in our minds.

These two factors can of course apply to any repeated piece of liturgy (the 23rd Psalm, or the Lord's Prayer, for example) but thirdly, hymns carry an added power in the music. Music works at a less cerebral level to affect our emotions and mood. Words become wedded to familiar and well-loved tunes; just think of the outcry if an organist or leader of worship tries to introduce a new tune to a well-loved hymn!

And finally, singing is an embodied and usually (apart from singing in the bath!) a corporate act. We stand as a body of people, as a group, using our bodies and our breath, in order to sing.

For all these reasons, hymns have a power to move and inspire us. But like symbolic action, they are performative ; they do not only express our emotions, our faith and our theology, they are constructive. Years ago the principal of my theological college told us, 'Congregations get most of their theology from the hymn book' and over the years I have come to realise how right he was! This means that the choice of hymns is important; we can absorb theological ideas and images without consciously questioning them, or hymns can stretch and challenge our understanding. Many contemporary hymns seek to do just that, and technology makes it easy for us to access and use new material.

Sharing the Word

What about the place of the Bible in worship? We talk of services of Word and Sacrament, and we will look at the sacrament of the Eucharist, or Holy Communion, in the next chapter, but the reading and exposition of the Bible plays a large part in most services of worship.

Many churches follow a lectionary, in order to ensure that major books and themes of Scripture are covered throughout the church year, rather than depending on the inspiration (or whim or hobby-horse!) of the preacher. For some, however, this is seen as placing constraints on the freedom of the Spirit, or the ability of the preacher to discern what is most relevant for a specific congregation on a particular occasion. The selection of lectionary passages in itself can have some serious omissions; difficult or challenging passages can be ignored. Sometimes the links between passages can be obscure and difficult to see.

In addition to the reading of Scripture, many questions are raised for progressive Christians. Preaching can seem a didactic, authoritarian mode of engaging with Biblical passages. However, it need not be so. A skilled preacher can retell the story, incorporating the insights of critical scholarship, in a way that invites a congregation on a journey of discovery. Preaching can be inductive, rather than deductive, helping people to find meaning in passages or text that they can apply and work with in their own lives. Alternative forms of worship, such as cafe-style worship, may well be experimenting with different ways of engaging with the biblical texts.

Preaching need not be the only way of engaging with Scripture. Bible studies, discussions, all-age activities that work with particular images or stories, can enable people to engage with biblical passages in new ways. Other readings, stories, and resources such as film or music may be used too, to engage people's imagination and bring the message to life. What is important is that however it happens, a dialogue opens up between the experience of the people and the biblical text, allowing questions to be raised and meaning to emerge.

Conclusion

The language of worship takes many forms in prayers and hymns, music and preaching, stories and images. What is needed for our worship to be contextual, relevant and inclusive is a creative and playful approach, and a willingness to try out new ways, words and images to bring worship to life.

Questions for discussion

1. Are there occasions when you have felt excluded, alienated or untouched in worship?

2. What helps to give you a sense of engagement or being included?

3. What is your favourite hymn, and why have you chosen it? Now look carefully at the words; how closely do they express your faith and theology?

Suggestion for worship or prayer

Write your own prayer. It may be one of thanks, or confession, or a prayer of concern for the needs of others. You may like to include a simple response that others can join in.

4. Sharing at the Table

Most of our traditions of worship (with the exception of the Quakers and the Salvation Army) include, in some form or another, the sacrament of sharing bread and wine. Whether it is referred to as Holy Communion or Eucharist, the Lord's Supper or the Breaking of Bread, sharing bread and wine in obedience to the words of Jesus at the Last Supper is seen as a central act of worship. It is in most Christian traditions regarded as a sacrament and a command from Jesus, and so should be a sign of unity. Yet it has probably caused more division, in terms of its significance, who can preside and who can partake, than any other Christian practice.

I do not want in this chapter to rehearse the arguments about transubstantiation, consubstantiation, real presence or memorial meal, nor the arguments about the authority to preside. Rather I want to explore how, whatever our tradition, we can find meaning which is consistent with an open, questioning approach to faith, and which will allow us to share at the table with integrity. This is something that not all of us find easy.

The language of sacrifice so often associated with communion, the imagery of the blood of Christ, implies for many a substitutionary understanding of atonement in which an angry deity (the Father) needs to be placated and reconciled with humanity through the sacrificial death of an innocent victim (His Son). Such imagery is difficult if not offensive to many within progressive Christianity. However, it is not the only way of understanding what we are doing when we share bread and wine.

The power of memory

We can begin with the idea of memory – which is embedded in the familiar words of the narrative of the institution (I Corinthians 11:23-26) and the Gospel stories. For some traditions this is the central meaning of this meal; it is a memorial, carried out in obedience to Christ. For others this is to reduce it to a 'mere memorial'. We need, however, to do full justice to the weight given to the word 'remember' in the biblical languages. To remember is not simply to look back and to recall, but to live something again, to re-present it in such a way that we are reliving the original experience. This is the sense in which the Jewish people remember the Passover, as if they too are living through that experience of liberation and freedom. When God remembers his people in the OT texts, such remembrance involves action; it is the prelude to

24

God's saving activity. So when we remember the life and death of Jesus in communion we are not simply recalling the story - we are placing ourselves within it. So the death and resurrection becomes not a once-for-all sacrifice, but an ongoing picture of God's mission in the world, a mission which we become part of when we share bread and wine.

Cross and resurrection

What does it mean to talk of the death and resurrection of Jesus in the world today? If we are to reject the idea of a once-for-all sacrifice, how do we interpret the cross?

On the cross many Christians see God suffering in Christ. For them this is not a once-for-all event, but can be a picture of how God shares in the suffering of the world: the brokenness of the bread represents the brokenness of humanity, the shed blood reminds us of the violence of wars and abuse. When we speak of the body and blood of Christ, we are speaking of a God who is Emmanuel, God-with-us in the suffering of the world. When we share in the bread and wine, we are affirming our solidarity with those who suffer and are oppressed.

The sacrament of Communion also includes a celebration of resurrection: it is Eucharist, a thanksgiving. So whilst we remember the suffering of the world, we also proclaim the hope of resurrection, that somehow, now in our present living and witness but not yet fully realised, love is stronger than hate, life stronger than death.

A shared meal

The meal that Jesus shares with his friends in the Gospel stories has its roots in the Passover - a celebration of liberation. So the bread and wine we share has a political dimension to it; it is a proclamation of liberation and justice. It recalls too other meals Jesus shared - with the sinners and the tax-gatherers, those who were marginalised and excluded. So the Eucharist should be a meal of inclusion – when we gather around the table the invitation is, or should be (!) open to all. It is a table of welcome and hospitality.

It is also a table at which we share; Communion is a corporate act. Although in some traditions it has been common in the past to talk of 'making my communion', increasingly partaking of the bread and wine is seen not as an individualistic act of devotion, but as relational, bringing people together around a table.

Sometimes this will be expressed in the layout of the building, with an altar placed in the centre of the congregation, or with the community gathered around a table. The sharing of the peace expresses this too; we cannot come to the table unless we have first made peace with one another. As one body, we share in the body of Christ. Just as the death of Jesus is embodied in the suffering of the world, so the life and mission of Jesus is embodied in the community of faith. The bread that we break is for us the body of Christ, but as we partake of that bread, so we renew ourselves as the body of Christ. Christ is incarnated (embodied, made flesh) in our living as we share the bread which is his body, and go out into the world to share the welcome, the grace and the justice of Christ.

A sacramental act

Communion, or Eucharist, is often referred to as a sacrament, an act in which God is uniquely present, and in which God's grace is conveyed. One of the reasons Quakers do not observe Communion is that for them every meal is a sacrament. There is a strength in this assertion; just as God is in every place, so God is present in every relationship, in every meal, at every table. But just as some places become special and sacred, so the everyday act of sharing food and drink, when carried out consciously and intentionally, becomes sacred for us.

Symbolic acts can be performative: they bring about the state that they signify. Because sharing bread and wine is a powerful, embodied symbolic act, it has the power to recreate us as the body of Christ. However we understand the activity of the Spirit in the sharing of bread and wine, as Christians we affirm that God is present in a particular way. The bread and wine become for us the body and blood of Christ.

There is a sense in which we can see the whole universe as sacramental. Every part of creation, every human relationship, every human activity has the potential to convey something of the presence and grace of God. By taking an everyday activity - eating and drinking together - we focus that presence of God in a particular embodied act.

Conclusion

Much of the language and imagery associated with Communion, or Eucharist, draws on a sacrificial world view. But if we focus on the roots in Passover and the simple act of friends sharing food together, we are drawn into a communal meal of hospitality, solidarity, justice and hope. Finding language and imagery that can express this is a major challenge for contemporary progressive liturgy.

Questions/further reflection

1. What do the various terms for sharing bread and wine (Eucharist, Communion, Lord's Supper, Memorial) mean to you? Which do you find most helpful, and why?

2. In your own tradition, how inclusive is the practice of sharing bread and wine?

Suggestion for worship or prayer

Take a piece of bread and break it, sharing it with others if you are in a group. As you do so, remember situations where you see God sharing in the suffering of the world. Turn these thoughts into prayer in whatever way is helpful for you; this may be silence, spoken words or a simple spoken or sung response.

Construct a form of communion that would work in your own context.

5. Conclusion: Transforming our Worship

In this booklet I have tried to set out ways of understanding the corporate worship of the church which will help progressive Christians find meaning and significance in this central activity of the community of faith. There are ways of sharing in worship and prayer which can be honest and enable us to retain our integrity; we can be inclusive and welcoming, developing a sense of community and belonging; we can leave worship feeling encouraged and uplifted for our daily living.

Our worship can be inclusive, liberating, playful and imaginative. But all too often we are stuck with a tradition of worship which is resistant to change, and which feels stifling and oppressive. How do we begin to transform our worship so that it becomes transformative of our life and faith?

Liturgy as the people's work.

If you are in a situation where you have some responsibility and freedom for the pattern of worship, for example if you are ordained, or a lay preacher or leader of worship, then this is a relatively simple process. There are any number of resources for worship (see the resources page for some suggestions) and with the modern technology of the internet, photocopier and data projector they can easily be made available to the congregation (although do beware of copyright restrictions and the need for appropriate acknowledgement).

Of course there will be resistance. Sometimes it is more effective to move slowly, introducing one new element at a time, but keeping something that is familiar (new words of a hymn to an existing tune for example, or a discussion instead of a sermon, but within the usual structure and framework). Special services celebrating the major Christian festivals, or all-age worship, can also offer opportunities for experimenting with more creative forms of worship.

The movement to create 'fresh expressions' of church, as part of our mission, can also offer opportunities. Sadly, some forms of this are simply doing the same old thing in a different setting, but alternative worship, cafe church, messy church and Godly play are all seeking to engage people in worship that will be creative, relevant and inclusive. Not all 'fresh expressions' will have a theology that is congruent with progressive Christianity, but many, in seeking to reach people outside the church, are rethinking language and imagery in a way that is also helpful to many dissatisfied with traditional forms.

Community or exodus?

What if you are in a situation where the liturgy is fixed, and there is resistance to any change? Sometimes people remain in such a situation for the sake of community; relationships have been formed over the years, and memories are strong. That sense of belonging can sustain us in spite of words and images that seem irrelevant or outdated. Sometimes the liturgy can carry us in that awareness of other people's faith: the communion of saints extended in time and space, regardless of our individual questions and doubts.

Sometimes it is possible to find opportunities to influence the pattern of worship – by introducing new hymns or different practices for intercessory prayers for example – or to find opportunities for prayer outside the main corporate worship of your church, in prayer groups or 'fresh expressions'. It may be possible to find ways of exploration and creativity that can go alongside the more traditional patterns.

For some, however, remaining in a pattern of worship that feels irrelevant, exclusive, or even oppressive, ceases to be an option. Many women have left the church because they can no longer tolerate exclusive language and the dominance of male imagery. The imagery of exodus, of leaving something that is restrictive and oppressive, is powerful; but for many, as in the biblical narrative, exodus leads to a wilderness, wandering without a fixed point of reference. That can be freeing, but also disorientating, often leading to a sense of isolation.

So people may turn to those traditions that allow more freedom in worship and less insistence on formal adherence to dogma, such as the Quakers, with their silence in meeting, and their commitment to justice and peace, or to the Unitarians, with their emphasis on individual understanding and conscience. Sometimes people will keep their allegiance to their own community of faith, but take opportunities to worship elsewhere as and when they can.

Others will find that sense of connection in nature, or in the creative arts – poetry or music, painting or sculpture. Finding moments of awareness and presence outside of church can sometimes help us to sustain regular or occasional church attendance for the sake of community, whilst our own spirituality is nourished elsewhere.

Worship in spirit and in truth

However we seek to worship, and however we understand that word, it remains important for us to keep our integrity. Those who lead worship have a particular responsibility to be true to their own convictions, but also to ensure that worship will not alienate or exclude others. Worship that is not true to our deepest convictions, that does not fire our passion for justice, that is not honouring of the glimpses of the divine we see in the world, will not sustain us. We need to worship in spirit and in truth.

Questions for discussion or reflection

1. Can you think of one thing in the regular worship of your own tradition that you would like to change? Can you see any possibilities for doing this?

2. Are there any ways in which you could influence the pattern of worship in your own context?

3. If you feel there are no possibilities for change, what is it that keeps you within that particular congregation or community of faith?

Suggestions for worship or prayer

Find an opportunity to participate in a form of worship that is unfamiliar to you. If you are part of a group, reflect together on the experience afterwards. Is there anything from this tradition of worship that you could learn from or incorporate into your own practice?

References

Northup, L. (1997). *Ritualizing Women*. Cleveland, Ohio: The Pilgrim Press.

Tillich, P. (1957). *Dynamics of Faith*. New York: Harper and Row.

Jan Berry's publications include:

'From Privacy to Prophecy' in *The Faith Lives of Women and Girls,* ed. Nicola Slee, Anne Phillips and Fran Porter, Ashgate 2013

Naming God, Granary Press URC/Magnet, 2011

Ritual Making Women: Shaping rites for changing lives, Equinox 2009

Prayers and worship material by Jan Berry in various anthologies, including Wild Goose Publications (see below). Also:

Wrestling and Resting: Exploring stories of spirituality from Britain and Ireland ed. Ruth Harvey CTBI 1999

Gateways of Grace ed. J Lees URC Prayer Handbook 1998-99

Human Rites: Worship Resources for an Age of Change ed. H Ward & J Wild Mowbray 1995

Celebrating Women ed. H Ward, J Wild, & J Morley SPCK 1995

Reflecting Praise ed. J Boyce-Tillman & J Wootton WIT/Stainer & Bell 1993

Bread of Tomorrow ed. J Morley Christian Aid/SPCK 1992

For further reading:

Burns, Stephen SCM *Studyguide: Liturgy,* London: SCM 2006

Day, Juliette & Gordon-Taylor, Benjamin (ed) *The Study of Liturgy and Worship,* London: SPCK 2013

Giles, Richard *Times and Seasons: creating transformative worship throughout the year* Norwich: Canterbury Press 2008

Giles, RichardCreating *Uncommon Worship: transforming the liturgy of the Eucharist,* Norwich: Canterbury Press 2004

Giles, Richard *Re-pitching the Tent,* Norwich: Canterbury Press 1999

White, Susan *Groundwork of Christian Worship* Peterborough: Epworth Press 1997

Resources for use in worship

Burgess, Ruth (ed) – series of anthologies from Wild Goose Publications, Iona Community, www.ionabooks.com

> *Hay and Stardust: Resources for Christmas to Candlemas*
>
> *Candles and Conifers: Resources for All Saints' and Advent*
>
> *Eggs and Ashes: Practical and liturgical resources for Lent and Holy Week*
>
> *Fire and Bread: Resources for Easter Day to Trinity Sunday*
>
> *Bare Feet and Buttercups: Resources for Ordinary Time*
>
> *Acorns and Archangels: Resources for Ordinary Time (The Feast of the Transfiguration to All Hallows)*
>
> *Moments of our nights and days (Liturgies and resources for baptisms, weddings, partnerships, friendships and the journey of life)*
>
> *Saying Goodbye: Resources for funerals, scattering ashes and remembering*

McBeath Clare & Presswood Tim *Crumbs of Hope: Prayers from the City* Peterborough: Inspire 2006

McEwan, Dorothy, et al *Making Liturgy: Creating Rituals for Worship and Life* Norwich: Canterbury Press 2001

McRae-McMahon, Dorothy:

Liturgies for Daily life London: SPCK 2004

Liturgies for High Days London: SPCK 2006 *and others*

Morley, Janet *All Desires Known (3rd ed)* London: SPCK 2005

Pratt Andrew and Dobson Marjorie *Nothing Too Religious: Worship Resources...but Nothing Too Religious* Inspire 2008

Collections of hymns by Fred Kaan, John Bell, Andrew Pratt, June Boyce-Tillman and other contemporary hymn and song writers can be purchased via various online booksellers

Collections of hymns and songs from Wild Goose publications – see www.ionabooks.com

Liturgies and prayers by Rex Hunt, a leading Australian progressive minister and writer can be found at: http://www.rexaehuntprogressive.com

Mainstream downloadable worship resources (which incur charges) from: www.theworshipcloud.com

The websites of the Together in Hope sponsoring organisations Modern Church and PCN Britain also have liturgy resources which you may find helpful.